108 RECIPES

GOURMET
VEGETARIAN
COOKING
from
NYINGMA
INSTITUTE

Nyingma Institute

Published by and available from
Nyingma Institute
1815 Highland Place, Berkeley, CA 94709
(510) 843-6812

ISBN 0-9639130-0-X

108 is an auspicious number in the Buddhist tradition

Illustrations courtesy of Sandra Benz, Robert Hartzema,
Steve Shumway, Melissa Lyckberg, and Eric Meller

Featured on the cover: Mango Soup without the Mango

Table of Contents

This book is dedicated to

TARTHANG TULKU,

who came to the United States, became a citizen,

and has worked unceasingly

to bring the teachings of

wisdom and compassion

to the West

Preface

U pon a full moon day in May 1993, the inspiration for publishing a cookbook suddenly appeared. Perhaps it was the *Wall Street Journal's* praise of our mango soup, or the continual procession of workshop participants filing into the kitchen to request the recipe for the dish they just loved, or simply the fact that after twenty years of great vegetarian cooking, the time was now ripe for publishing some of our favorite recipes.

The Nyingma Institute was founded in 1973. Under the guidance of Tarthang Tulku, a Tibetan lama of the Nyingma tradition, an old fraternity house was transformed into an innovative environment for Buddhist education and practice. When residential programs began, a full-blown kitchen sprang to life, and soon a variety of delicious vegetarian dishes were served regularly. Ever since, there has existed a long lineage of head cooks who have passed along their knowledge and experience. Also, a number of international students who have lived and studied with us have contributed recipes from their home countries, enriching our cuisine.

Over the years, the Nyingma Institute has gained a reputation for creative and satisfying vegetarian food. More importantly, though, the Institute kitchen has become a classroom for learning and developing such qualities as concentration, responsibility, and caring—a classroom for practicing awareness in everyday life.

Introduction

What is gourmet cuisine? At its best, rather than being limited to exotic, elaborate creations, gourmet cooking is a matter of simple, high quality ingredients prepared with attention and care.

Making rich food taste great is relatively easy. The real art is to prepare a feast without the use of expensive ingredients flown in from the other side of the world, and without having to spend three days at the stove. As the Chinese masters of old used to say, the true art is to make a broth of wild grasses taste as good as a fine cream soup.

Anyone can develop this skill. There is nothing genetic or mystical about it. Skill in cooking comes from cultivating an alive and sensitive interest in the process. All you need is a willingness to be open to the experience, and courage to follow wherever it takes you.

Humility and patience will also help. No one can make an eggplant bake faster than it will, or persuade a turnip to taste like a sweet potato (I tried once). The ingredients and processes we use in the kitchen are rich and wonderful and exactly what they are, and we did not invent them. By working with a sensitive mind and an open heart, it is possible to gain direct access to the creative resources of the universe, and so to serve as a means through which its gifts can flow to others.

It is simple—but not always easy. Cooking is a continuous practice in awareness. When you prepare meals, what is the quality of your mind? What relationship do you have to the ingredients? In addition to the Belgian endive, what are you offering your family and guests? Appreciation, sensitivity, and creativity—or is it sometimes boredom, anxiety, frustration?

Whenever my mind is scattered—wanting to be elsewhere, replaying past dramas and rehearsing the future—not only do I end up with deep cuts in my left thumb, but also the food does not taste as good. Even the "surefire" recipes do not seem to work. But when I am present and interested in whatever I am doing, even the most mundane activity can be a source of inspiration and joy.

Magic and beauty can be found in the simplest things. All we need to do is to wake up to this possibility. (Have you ever seen a cauliflower? I mean, have you really *seen* it?) While you cook, stop for a moment to admire the shape and color of a red bell pepper, the smell of fresh basil, the texture of barley grains. When you look carefully, the shades and reflexes of pinto beans glimmering in the water can seem like semi-precious stones. Such moments of sensitive enjoyment will inspire you and make you capable of nourishing both the bodies and the spirits of those who will eat your food.

Let all your senses be open while you work. Feel your way, and listen to what the ingredients have to tell you. Once you have cooked a few recipes with carrots, you can begin to intuit what they like to have in their company: ginger, for example, or tarragon, dill, lemon butter, almonds. Such knowledge arises from your own experience, and it becomes the inspiration for creating your own recipes as well as for interpreting and enhancing those received from elsewhere.

In this cookbook, some recipes give hints instead of exact measures, especially for spices. After all, how can anybody know how much salt *you* like in your pasta sauce? Any recipe can, in fact, be considered a theme upon which to improvise. So when there *are* exact measures, please do not let these discourage you from experimentation. How do you think great recipes come into being?

Whatever you observe, consider writing it down. For example, make notes in the margins of the recipes you try: what you changed, what you wish you hadn't, what you'd like to do next time, and whatever else you noticed: the baking dish doesn't need so much oil, the parsley lost its flavor by being added so soon, the lime juice made a wonderful contrast, and so on.

Sometimes it can happen that you choose a recipe and plan your lunch around it, and then at the last minute you discover that you are missing one or two ingredients. In such a case, the procedure is as follows: Set aside your self-importance. Let go of needing the outcome to be perfect. Maintain the attitude of relaxed curiosity—and then go ahead, and use the recipe anyway. You can always omit, substitute, simulate, or make do. (I hope what you lack will be the less essential items, although Mango Soup without the Mango really is quite excellent.)

This situation invites you to imagine the combination of remaining ingredients, sense the role the missing ones would have played, and allow your mind to be an open space within which ideas can arise of what could fill the gap. It's a wonderful stimulus to sensitivity, creativity, and learning, and you may even improve on the original recipe.

Finally, remember that cooking is not about following recipes—and not even about creating your own. Cooking is an act of generosity and caring, and an opportunity to appreciate life's gifts. That is the spirit in which this book has been written. My hope is that, rather than being just another collection of recipes, it will inspire you toward a new approach to cooking.

Enjoy your meal. Enjoy your life.

Zuza (Jolanta Kusa)
Berkeley, Fall 1993

Acknowledgements

This cookbook is more than the creation of an individual. As practicing within a supportive community is fundamental to Buddhism, this book too is a result of cooperation of many people from throughout the world.

I express my deep gratitude to Tarthang Tulku, Rinpoche, for creating the Institute as an environment for living and practice; to Fred and Abbe with whom I first learned how to cook a multi-course gourmet meal for a crowd in an hour and a half, and to breathe at the same time; and to Frances who taught me all I needed to know about how to run the kitchen (and my life); and to all the others who have contributed recipes and insights from their own experience.

I would also like to acknowledge the influence other cookbooks had on my cuisine: in particular, such classics as *Moosewood, Silver Palate*, and *Greens*.

Last but not least, one hundred-and-eight-thousand thanks to the staff of the Institute for their unwavering support for this project: especially to Barry Schieber, Dean of the Institute, without whose enthusiasm this book would never have seen the light, and to Eric Meller who with unrelenting diligence translated enthusiasm into printed text.

108 RECIPES

GOURMET
VEGETARIAN
COOKING
from
NYINGMA
INSTITUTE

✦ CHAPTER 1 ✦

*A*ppetizers

As its name suggests, an appetizer is meant to stimulate interest in the rest of the menu. Therefore, it should be something small, assertive, visually appealing, perhaps even a little intriguing. (Celery and carrot sticks with the same old dip just do not quite meet this requirement.)

Apart from being a tasty introduction to the meal, an appetizer can fulfill other practical functions. It gives the cook time to breathe before the grand evening really begins, helps win some time in case of a serious delay in the kitchen, entertains those who were insensitive enough to show up early, and averts attention from those who come late.

You can begin your dinner party by walking among your guests with trays of bite-sized toasts with various toppings. Make tiny toasts from fancy thin baguettes, or use thin, crisp, unusual crackers. The toppings can range from a simple cheese-and-herb spread to the most elaborate concoctions. For starters, you can try the Eggplant Provençal, the Artichoke Dip, or Abbe's Pesto.

Even if you use just one topping, make each tray *look* different. Decorate the toasts with bits of red or yellow peppers, red radishes, tomatoes, olives, nuts, fresh and dried herbs, marinated mushrooms, cocktail onions, pickles, or capers. Use anything edible (including flowers) that can add color or texture.

If you are planning a more formal, sit-down meal, a wonderful way to set the tone for the evening is to have the table set with individual appetizer plates. Again the possibilities for creativity are endless. Surprise yourself. Combine flavors you have never had together, and colors that make a stunning effect.

Many marinated vegetables are excellent as part of an appetizer plate. Look for inspiration in recipes like Marinated Vegetable Salad or Salade en Brochettes. Better yet, invent your own marinades—and do not forget fancy vinegars, interestingly flavored mustards, and fresh herbs such as savory, oregano, and mint. Some of the gourmet condiments are expensive, but usually they are worth the investment. Often, a small quantity will go a long way—and really make a difference.

Arrange pieces of vegetables and fruits, marinated or raw, on fresh leaves of Belgian endive, radicchio, or Boston lettuce. Add a dab of guacamole or some tofu spread, or both. Almost anything with an assertive taste can be used, including pickles of all sorts, balanced with some more neutral tasting ingredients, such as slices of papaya or raw mushrooms. Serve some light bread or crackers on the side.

One way to create harmony in your menu is to design the appetizers as a hint of the courses to come. This can be done by repeating an ingredient, spice, or color combination. For example, to "announce" a raspberry vinaigrette which will arrive later with the salad, include a few whole raspberries in the appetizer arrangement. This way of composing a meal will help make it into an integral whole.

Eggplant Provençal

from Zuza
serves 4–6 people

This wonderful spread can be served on tiny baguette toasts as an appetizer for an elegant party. Eggplant needs lengthy baking and cooling time—so plan ahead. The good news is that this dish gets better with time, so give it at least an overnight stay in your refrigerator before you serve it.

2	*eggplants*
5	*cloves garlic*
4 T	*olive oil*
3	*ripe Roma tomatoes, diced*
¼ c	*currants*
⅓ c	*fresh basil, finely chopped*
	salt and pepper, to taste
	splash of apple cider vinegar
¼ c	*chopped Italian parsley*
1	*very thin French or sourdough baguette (for toasts)*
	pine nuts (garnish)

Cut the eggplants in half lengthwise, and place them flat side up in a well-oiled baking dish. Peel the garlic, slice it thinly, and stuff it into the eggplant flesh. Brush the eggplants with olive oil. Cover the dish with foil, and bake at 375° for 60 minutes, or until the eggplants are very soft.

Set the eggplants aside until they are cool enough to handle. Scrape the flesh and garlic into a small bowl, adding the oil from the pan. Mash with a fork, and add all the other ingredients *except* the parsley, bread, and nuts.

Mix well, season to taste, and refrigerate overnight. Before serving, stir in the parsley, then taste to adjust seasoning.

To make the toast, preheat the oven to 400°. Cut the baguette in 1" slices on the diagonal, and toast on a buttered cookie sheet in the oven for 5 to 7 minutes, until golden brown. Let cool slightly. Spread the eggplant paste thickly on the little toasts, and garnish with toasted pine nuts or toasted chopped almonds.

Auch's Artichoke Dip

from Len Hilgerman
serves 6–8 people

1	can (about 17 oz) unmarinated artichoke hearts
1 c	mayonnaise
1	small can (about 7 oz) diced green chiles
1 c	Parmesan cheese, grated
1	loaf Milano bread
1	can or jar of salsa

Cut the artichoke hearts into eighths, or bite-sized pieces. Mix with the mayonnaise, peppers, and Parmesan cheese. Pour into a 9" square baking dish. Bake at 325° for 15 to 20 minutes, or until brown.

Slice the bread thinly, and toast it in the oven on both sides. Serve with the dip and salsa. Taco chips can be used in place of the bread.

Basil Pesto without Pine Nuts

from Abbe Blum
makes 1½ cups

This pesto is less fatty and less expensive than most, but no less intense. Serve it as an appetizer on tiny baguette toasts (see Eggplant Provençal), decorated with French black olives. It can also be used as a sauce for pasta or boiled new potatoes.

9	*medium to large cloves of garlic*
½ c	*walnuts*
5–6 T	*grated Parmesan, or more to taste*
¼ c	*olive oil*
½	*salt*
	black pepper, to taste
2–3 T	*hot water*
1	*large bunch of fresh basil, washed, large stems removed*
1	*bunch of Italian parsley, top part only (reserve stems for soup stock)*

In a food processor, grind the garlic into very small pieces. Add half the olive oil and all the walnuts, and blend into a paste. Scrape the sides once or twice. Add the basil, parsley, salt, pepper, and a few tablespoons of the hot water. Process until very smooth. Drizzle in the remaining oil. Fold in the Parmesan.

Note: Before the Parmesan is added, the pesto can be frozen in a little olive oil for storage.

Baked Pears Stuffed with Gorgonzola and Walnuts

from Zuza
serves 6 people

Pears stuffed with cheese and nuts are served as a dessert in France. This version varies from the traditional French recipe in that the pears are baked before (and after) they are stuffed. They can be served as part of a fancy meal—for example with Oven Roasted Vegetables, Wild Rice with Nuts and Cranberries, and Fred's Mango Salad. You can add another treat for dessert—but perhaps not the French Pear Pie!

3	*pears (half a pear per person), medium-ripe —e.g., D'Anjou, bartlett, or red blush pears*
2 T	*butter*
3 T	*dry sherry*
⅓ c	*walnuts, roughly chopped*
9 oz	*Gorgonzola*

Preheat the oven to 350°. Wash the pears, cut them in half lengthwise, and core them with an apple corer or a sharp teaspoon, giving each a large cavity in which to put the stuffing. Prepare a shallow glass baking dish by putting a dot of butter on the bottom of it for each pear half. Place the pears in the dish, the flat surface facing down, and splash with sherry. Bake for 10–12 minutes, until tender but firm.

Meanwhile, prepare the stuffing. In a small bowl, crumble the Gorgonzola. Toast the walnuts over a low flame in a dry skillet, stirring constantly. Combine the walnuts with the cheese while they are still hot—the heat will soften the cheese, making the two ingredients stick together better.

Remove the pears from the oven and allow them to cool slightly, then turn them over in the baking dish. Form the cheese-nut mixture into small balls with your fingers, and stuff one into the cavity of each pear, pressing lightly.

Right before serving, return the pears to the oven, broiling them for a few minutes until the cheese has melted some. Serve either hot or at room temperature.

Spinach Appetizers

from Len Hilgerman
makes 30 balls

2	10 oz boxes of frozen, chopped spinach
3 c	herb-seasoned stuffing mix
1	large onion, very finely chopped
6	eggs, well beaten
¾ c	butter, melted
½ c	Parmesan cheese, grated
1 t	pepper
1½ t	garlic salt (or 1 t grated fresh garlic plus ½ t salt)
1½ t	thyme (amount can be adjusted to blend well with the flavor of the stuffing mix)

Cook the spinach, drain it, and squeeze out the water. Combine with the other ingredients, and mix thoroughly. Grease your hands, and shape the mixture into 1" balls. Place these on a lightly greased cookie sheet. Sprinkle a little more cheese over the top, and bake in a 325° oven for 15 to 20 minutes, or until lightly brown on top.

Toast with Feta and Hummus

from Zuza
serves 4–6 people

1½ c   *Hummus (recipe on page 125)*
12   *slices whole wheat bread, cut in half on the diagonal (making triangles)*
           butter
3   *ripe tomatoes, sliced*
12 oz   *Feta cheese, crumbled or finely sliced*
12   *Greek black olives*
           fresh Italian parsley leaves, for garnish

Preheat the oven to 400°. Butter the bread slices, and place them buttered side down on a baking sheet. Spread a generous amount of hummus on each. Arrange the tomato slices on top, sprinkle with the feta, and decorate with olives.

Bake for 10 minutes at 400°. Remove from the oven, garnish with parsley leaves, and serve immediately.

These can be made in advance, to patiently await their turn in the oven.

✦ CHAPTER 2 ✦

Soups

Half the secret of a delicious soup is the quality of your soup stock. The other half must be some mysterious transmission of wisdom from generations past. I know in my case the women in my family never taught me to make soups, yet I always knew how. So never underestimate your family heritage. Even if you think you have no clue how Mom or Dad made their minestrone or matzo ball soup, you do know how it *should* taste. Let that knowledge guide you on your path of discovery.

You *could* substitute water for stock in all the recipes, but if you do, you should not expect too much from your soups. Stock is easy to make if you dedicate yourself to saving vegetable scraps over a few days. This does not include, however, wilted or rotten parts, or anything at all approaching that description. It's simple: good ingredients make good stock.

Good things for creating a stock include:

- ✦ *peeled onions (best when first slightly charred directly over a flame)*
- ✦ *carrot and potato skins and pieces*
- ✦ *celery root (scrubbed clean and chopped) and root parsley*
- ✦ *eggplant, zucchini, celery, tomato chunks*
- ✦ *chunks of any winter squash (include the skins and seeds)*
- ✦ *lettuce leaves, herb stems and leaves*
- ✦ *mushrooms, fresh and dried*
- ✦ *whole cloves of garlic, unpeeled*

I do not recommend cauliflower, cabbage, onion peels, broccoli, or Brussels sprouts because their flavors are too strong.

To make the stock, put all the ingredients into a large soup pot, along with a bay leaf or two and several whole grains of allspice. Cover with cold water, bring to a boil, and let simmer over a very low flame for 1 to 2 hours. Then strain and refrigerate. Use the stock within the next few days.

To make a vegetarian soup, one common and excellent way to begin is to sauté an onion in a little oil or butter. Then add the other vegetables of your choice. At that point, you can either continue sautéing before adding your stock, or add the stock immediately.

Beans make great soups—but if you are using dry beans, remember to soak them in cold water, preferably overnight (only lentils can be cooked without soaking). Soaking cuts the cooking time and makes the beans easier to digest. Putting a peeled onion in with the soaking water may help, too. Supposedly, the onion draws from the beans the substances that would give digestive trouble—but then the onion contains them in a concentrated form, so remember to discard it along with the soaking liquid before cooking the beans. To cook the beans, cover them generously with fresh cold water, and add a bay leaf. Do not add salt until the very end of the cooking time. Include the cooking liquid in your soup—it adds body and flavor.

Always remember to taste your soup before you serve it. The flavor of some herbs and spices may be lost during cooking if they are added early, so you'll need to correct the seasonings. The addition of cream will also steal some flavor, especially spicyness. Lemon juice enhances flavors, and sometimes it makes a good substitute for salt. Almost every soup will gain in flavor and character if you sprinkle it with fresh herbs before you serve it. Experiment with Italian parsley, scallions, dill, fresh basil, tarragon, cilantro, or marjoram.

Mushroom-Barley Soup

from Zuza
serves 4–6 people

½ c	dry sherry
8	dried mushrooms
8 c	vegetable stock, or more, as needed
½ c	dry barley
1	bay leaf
1	large onion, chopped
1	clove garlic, chopped
1 lb	fresh mushrooms, coarsely chopped
2 T	butter
1 T	olive oil
¼ c	tamari, or more to taste
	salt and pepper, to taste
1 T	apple cider vinegar
¼ c	Italian parsley, finely chopped
	dark sesame oil

In a small saucepan, heat the sherry along with the dried mushrooms until almost boiling, remove from the flame, and let the mushrooms soak for at least half an hour.

In a small pot, bring to boil 3 cups of stock with the barley and bay leaf. Cover and let simmer for 45 minutes or more, until the barley is barely tender; it should still be firm and chewy.

Meanwhile, chop the onions, garlic, and fresh mushrooms. In the soup pot, heat the butter and oil, and sauté the onions along with the garlic until the onions are translucent.

At this point you can add the fresh mushrooms to the pot, and sauté them for 10–12 minutes. (If you have the time, sear the mushrooms first in a heavy skillet—with an additional 1 tablespoon of butter and ½ teaspoon salt—until they are crisp and golden, and then add to the onions. Make sure to deglaze the skillet to release the pan juices. Include those in your soup, too.)

Add the cooked barley with its liquid to the soup pot. Drain the wild mushrooms, and pour their sherry into the soup pot. Pour slowly, so any sediment will be left on the bottom of the saucepan. Sliver the mushrooms, and add these to the pot. Add tamari, salt, and pepper. Let the soup simmer, covered, for half an hour or so. Add the remaining 5 cups of stock, or more if the soup is too thick.

Before serving, add 1 tablespoon of apple cider vinegar. Taste—add one or two more splashes if needed, and correct the other seasonings. Stir in the parsley, and sprinkle with sesame oil. Serve very hot.

Squash Soup

from Iris Maitland
serves 2–4 people

1	*medium butternut squash*
3	*large acorn squashes*
	water
2 T	*butter*
1	*bunch of scallions*
	soy sauce, to taste

Scrub the squash, and cut it in large pieces without peeling. Put these in a medium soup pot, add water to cover, bring to a boil, and simmer gently until tender. Drain, reserving liquid. Meanwhile, sauté the scallions in butter. When the squash is cool enough to handle, scoop out the flesh. Puree in batches in a blender or a food processor, adding equal amounts of the cooking liquid, and all the scallions. Thin to desired consistency and season with soy sauce.

Clear Cauliflower Soup

from Zuza
serves 4–6 people

1	*small head cauliflower, separated in small florets*
3	*medium carrots, thickly sliced*
6 c	*vegetable stock*
3 T	*soy sauce, or to taste*
¼ c	*fresh parsley, chopped*
¼ c	*fresh dill, chopped*

This deceptively simple soup is quick to make and very light, but it tastes great! Bring the stock to a boil, add the vegetables, and cook until barely tender. Add herbs and season with soy sauce.

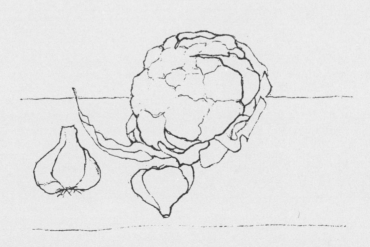

Lima Bean Soup in Primary Colors

from Zuza
serves 6–8 people

1 c	dried baby lima beans
6 c	water
1	bay leaf
2 T	olive oil
2	onions, sliced
1 c	carrots, peeled and diced
1	red bell pepper, diced
1	yellow bell pepper, diced
1 c	celery, finely chopped
¼ c	fresh dill, chopped
1	small head of anise, diced
1 T	salt
1 t	black pepper
6 c	vegetable stock (or water)
1 T	dried tarragon
3 T	fresh parsley, chopped
¾ c	black olives, sliced

This is a pretty soup with a comforting taste. Soak the beans overnight. Then change the water, add a bay leaf, and cook until barely tender, about 40 minutes. Heat the oil in a heavy soup pot, and sauté the onions until golden. Add carrots, peppers, celery, anise, dill, salt, and pepper. Sauté 8–10 minutes. Add the beans, their cooking liquid, and the stock (add more stock or water if soup is too thick). Cover. Simmer on medium flame until vegetables are tender. Add tarragon, parsley, and olives. Simmer 3 minutes. Adjust seasoning. Serve with bread, Brie, and green salad.

Cream of Asparagus Soup

from Mary Webster
serves 4–6 people

4	leeks, trimmed of greens (or a bunch of green onions)
2	cloves garlic
2½ lbs	asparagus, washed
6½ c	vegetable stock
4 T	butter or margarine
1 t	thyme, dried
2	bay leaves
1 c	cream
¼ t	nutmeg
	salt and pepper to taste
4	egg yolks
2 T	fresh dill, chopped

Chop the leeks and garlic together. Cut off the asparagus tips—then cut the rest in ½" chunks. Boil the tips 3 minutes in 1 cup of vegetable stock; then drain them and reserve the stock.

Melt the butter, and cook the leeks (or onions) and garlic about 5 minutes. Add the chopped asparagus stems, along with the thyme and bay leaves. Then add the reserved and remaining stock. Reduce the heat, and simmer for 30 minutes.

Remove the bay leaf, and puree. Return the puree to the pan. Add ¼ cup cream, the asparagus tips, the nutmeg, and the salt and pepper.

Mix the remaining cream with the yolks. Spoon some of the hot puree into the egg-cream mixture, then slowly add the rest, stirring constantly with a whisk no more than 3 minutes. Add a bit of milk if necessary. Serve sprinkled with dill.

Zuza's Borscht

from Zuza
serves 6 people

6	medium beets
1	sour apple, quartered
2 T	oil
1	medium yellow onion, halved and sliced
5	cloves garlic
1½ t	caraway seeds
2	carrots, peeled and sliced 1" thick
1	stalk of celery, chopped
4 c	vegetable broth, or more, as needed
3	medium potatoes, quartered
1 t	salt
1 t	pepper
3–4 T	apple cider vinegar
¼ c	fresh dill, chopped
¼ c	fresh Italian parsley, chopped
	a little brown sugar

Cut off the ends of the beets, and scrub thoroughly. Then cover the whole beets and the apple chunks with 6 cups water in a sturdy pot, and cook until tender; this may take up to 40 minutes. The acidity of the apple will help to preserve the bright color of the beet juice.

Heat the oil in a heavy soup pot and add the onions, sautéing until translucent. Add 3 cloves of crushed garlic and the caraway seeds; sauté for one more minute. Add carrots and celery, and sauté for 7–10 minutes. Then add 4 cups of vegetable broth, and the potatoes, salt, and pepper.

Bring to a boil, reduce the heat, and simmer for 20 minutes, or until all the vegetables are tender.

When the beets are done, cool them until they are ready to handle; then peel and cube them. Discard the apple. Add the beets and their cooking juice to the soup pot, and simmer gently 10 more minutes to blend the flavors. (Be careful—a furious boil will destroy the color.)

Add the fresh herbs, the vinegar, and an additional grind of pepper. Taste to correct the seasoning. If the soup tastes too sour, add a little brown sugar—just enough to cut the acidity. Add 2 cloves of pressed garlic. Serve the soup with sour cream and hard-boiled eggs.

Ukrainian Borscht

from Luda Osinovsky
serves 4–6 people

This balance of underground vegetables—the "cold", earthy, root ones, and the "hot", sunny ones—may make you feel that you are eating something substantial and at the same time are being nurtured by the sun.

½ c	dried kidney beans
6 c	water
2	medium potatoes, sliced
1	medium onion, chopped or sliced
2 T	vegetable oil
2 T	tomato paste
3	medium tomatoes, chopped
6	medium beets, peeled and cubed
2	medium carrots, sliced
½	red bell pepper, sliced
¼	medium cabbage, shredded
12	mushrooms, chopped
	seasonings, to your taste (salt, dried bay leaf, dried or fresh dill, parsley, garlic)
	Sour cream for garnish

Soak the beans in lukewarm water for 4 to 5 hours, until they swell. Drain and rinse. Put them into a stock pot with a quart of water, and bring to a boil. Boil 5 to 10 minutes. Then add 1 cup lukewarm water, and bring to a boil again. Repeat this one more time. Then add the onions and potatoes. Bring to a boil, reduce the heat, and simmer.

Meanwhile, heat the oil in a heavy skillet, and add the tomato paste, tomatoes, beets, carrots, and pepper. Fry until a light crust is formed. Then add the contents of the skillet to the stock pot.

Add the cabbage and mushrooms. After a minute or two, add salt and the other seasonings. Cover the pot tightly, reduce the heat to *low*, and simmer for 15 to 20 minutes.

Borscht may be served at once, but it is a good idea to keep it on the stove, without heat, for about ½ hour. Stir in some crushed garlic, and serve topped with a generous amount of sour cream.

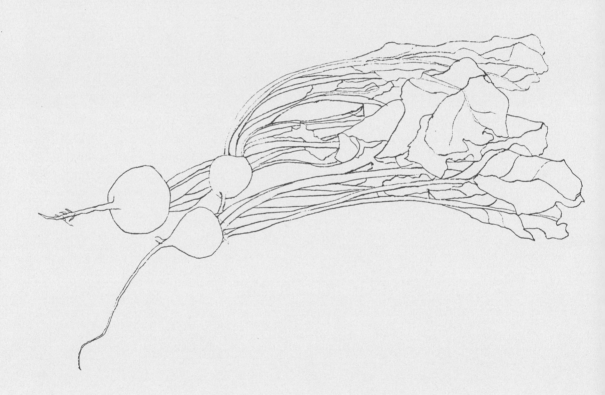

Black Bean Soup

from Zuza
serves 4–6 people

2 c	dried black beans
1	bay leaf
3 T	oil
2	yellow onions, chopped
5	cloves garlic, chopped
1 T	cumin seeds
1 T	dried oregano
1 T	paprika
¼ t	cayenne
1 lb	ripe tomatoes, chopped
2 T	chili powder
1 t	salt
1 t	canned chilpotle chili paste
1 qt	orange juice
1 qt	vegetable stock, or as needed
1 T	apple cider vinegar
¼ c	fresh cilantro, chopped

Soak the beans overnight, then drain and rinse. Cover with fresh water and add the bay leaf. Bring to a boil; reduce the heat, and simmer over a low flame for 20 minutes.

In a heavy soup pot, heat the oil. Add the onions and garlic, and sauté until translucent.

Meanwhile, roast the cumin seeds in a small skillet. When they begin to smell smoky, remove from heat, and add the oregano, paprika, and cayenne; shake the skillet for a few seconds. Grind these ingredients in a spice grinder. Add to the onions, along with the tomatoes, chili powder, salt, and chili paste. Simmer uncovered for 20 minutes.

When the beans are barely tender, add them to the soup pot along with the orange juice. Add enough vegetable stock to cover by at least one inch. Simmer for another ½ hour, adding stock as necessary.

Add vinegar and salt to taste. Add the cilantro, and serve with sour cream. Corn bread makes a nice accompaniment.

Red Lentil Dal

from Zuza
serves 4–6 people

Dhal is a generic name for an Indian lentil dish that is something like a thick lentil soup, but even better. Usually it is part of a multi-course meal. You can serve it with the Carrot or Banana Curry, Basmati rice, and a yogurt-drenched salad.

1 c	red lentils
1	bay leaf
2 qt	soup stock, or more as needed
2 T	vegetable oil
1 t	black mustard seeds
1	medium onion, coarsely chopped
6	whole cardamom pods, crushed with a wooden spoon
1 t	coriander, ground, or ½ t whole seeds
3 t	cumin, ground
1 t	turmeric, ground
½ t	ginger powder
3	medium carrots, finely diced
⅛–¼ t	cayenne, or more for those who like it hot
	salt, to taste
	soy sauce, to taste
2 T	chopped fresh parsley

Rinse the lentils. Then put them in a medium pot, along with the bay leaf and enough stock to cover. Bring to a boil, reduce the heat, and simmer for 10 minutes.

Meanwhile, heat the oil in a heavy stock pot. Add the mustard seeds, and heat until they begin to pop slightly. Then add the onion. After 5 minutes, add the other spices, plus the carrots; include ⅛ teaspoon cayenne, but wait until later before deciding whether to add more cayenne. Sauté the ingredients another 5 minutes, stirring often because the spices will want to stick to the bottom of the pot.

Add the lentils along with their liquid, and more stock if the soup is too thick. Add salt and soy sauce. Cover and let simmer for 20 minutes or more, depending on the desired degree of lentil disintegration. I like them cooked into oblivion, but if you are really particular about having this soup clear and the lentils whole, do not boil the lentils separately. Instead, add them raw with the stock when the carrots are barely tender, and then watch carefully. Red lentils are tricky—they can be hard one minute, and mush the next.

Taste the soup to correct the seasoning. Add any extra cayenne with mindfulness. Remember that it develops its heat over a few minutes—overdoing it will kill the wonderful taste of the lentils. Sprinkle with parsley before serving.

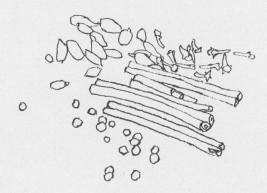

Mango Soup without the Mango

from Zuza
serves many people

This light, refreshing fruit soup was mentioned in the May 1992 *Wall Street Journal* article featuring the Institute's Continuing Education Programs. I had made the soup for lunch during one of our Stress Reduction programs for lawyers. The "mango soup" got as good a review as the workshop itself. Actually, there was no mango in that soup, but I liked the idea, so the next time I made it, I included some of that wonderful fruit. Exquisite.

Here's how to achieve an unusual creation. Really all it takes is a blender or food processor—and wild imagination. The secret of this soup is to make it differently each time, using whatever fruit is on hand. The addition of fresh mangoes makes it very special, of course, but even if all you have available are canned peaches, the result will be a pleasant surprise. Instead of a recipe, here are some basic guidelines:

Good fruits to consider as the base for this soup include melons, peaches, pineapples, papayas, very ripe pears, and mangoes—fruits with high water content and a distinct taste.

If you have fresh fruit, use only the best and ripest ones. You can also use canned peaches and pineapples; it is best to drain them and discard the syrup, which is usually much too sweet.

Fruit such as grapes or berries (strawberries, blackberries, blueberries) are very nice as garnish; in fact, it is worth an extra effort (and expense) to include some, for they make the appearance of the soup even more appetizing.

Kiwi fruit deserve special attention. Their acidity balances wonderfully with the sweetness of other fruit, and they are pretty too, so you can use them both for the base and as a garnish.

To make the soup, blend all the fruit together (except the garnish) in a food processor or blender. You will need some fresh lemon or lime juice to make it less sweet. Then look at your soup. If its consistency resembles that of applesauce, you'll want to dilute it. The best way to do this without compromising the taste is to use mineral water, orange juice, or grapefruit juice; other fruit juices can be an option, but are usually too sweet. You can also add some dry sherry at this point, in a quantity that seems appropriate to the occasion.

Now taste the soup and see what else it might need. If it is still too sweet, add more lemon juice.

Finely chopped fresh mint leaves are an excellent addition. If you like mint anyway and are *sure* you know how much of it you want, add it into the food processor when you are blending the fruit. Otherwise, chop some leaves and add them gradually, tasting as you go. Be careful—you might end up with mint soup. Remember that it takes a while for the flavors of herbs and spices to develop, especially in a cold dish, so you might want to reserve some of the mint to be added later, if necessary. This soup is best when it is allowed to chill for several hours; you can always adjust the seasonings right before serving.

Other spices to consider adding (in small quantities) include ground cloves, cinnamon, powdered ginger, fresh ginger (start with ½ teaspoon), and nutmeg.

When you are ready to serve, taste the soup one more time, and adjust the seasoning. Then ladle it into individual bowls, and garnish with whatever you have at hand: whole berries, black grapes, lemon wedges, whole mint leaves, flowers, currants, even toasted chopped almonds.

If you need a special effect for a spectacular start to your dinner, I recommend the following. Serve the soup with an abstract art look by painting delicate patterns on its orange surface with raspberry puree. To make the puree, blend 1 cup of fresh raspberries with 2 tablespoons of maple syrup and a splash of brandy. Reserve some whole raspberries and select a few small mint leaves to complete the garnish.

Cold Avocado Cream Soup

from Abbe Blum
serves 4–6 people

4 c	*vegetable stock (approximate)*
3	*avocadoes*
6 t	*lemon juice*
3 t	*cream cheese*
½ c	*yogurt*
¾ t	*salt*
1 t	*sugar*

Simple and pleasantly unusual. In a blender or food processor, puree the ingredients together in two batches. In each batch, first puree half the avocadoes, cream cheese, and lemon juice until smooth, then gradually add half the stock and yogurt. Combine the batches in a bowl, add the sugar and salt, and chill in a refrigerator. Serve garnished with thin slices of lemon.

Cold Cucumber Soup

from Zuza
serves 4–6 people

4	*cucumbers, peeled and coarsely chopped*
4 c	*yogurt or buttermilk*
	salt and pepper, to taste
1 T	*fresh mint, finely chopped*

Blend all ingredients together in a food processor. Taste to correct seasoning. Serve chilled. Easy enough?

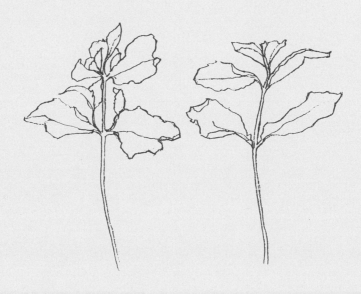

Oriental Spinach Soup

from Zuza
serves 4–6 people

This soup is fast and easy to make. Soaking the mushrooms does take a while, but you can use that time to prepare the other ingredients or another dish. The taste is rich and dark, and the soup is pretty with its deep green spinach leaves and black specks of mushroom.

10	dried shiitake mushrooms, soaked in hot water for ½ hour
2 T	dark sesame oil, plus some to sprinkle on top
2 t	vegetable oil
3	cloves garlic, crushed
1	bunch spinach, with stems, washed and coarsely chopped
6 c	vegetable stock, plus the soaking liquid from the mushrooms
½ t	salt
2 T	soy sauce, or more to taste
3 T	nutritional (brewer's) yeast flakes
	coarsely ground pepper

Drain the mushrooms, adding their liquid to the stock. Be sure to pour it carefully, leaving some on the bottom of the soaking bowl to avoid getting the fine sand often found in mushrooms into your stock. Sliver the mushrooms thinly. Heat the stock in a small pot, and have it ready at hand.

In a heavy soup pot, heat the sesame and vegetable oils. Add the garlic and mushrooms, and stir-fry for half a minute. Add the spinach, and sauté for 1 more minute, until the spinach has just wilted. Then add the hot stock, salt, soy sauce, and yeast, and let simmer for 10 minutes.

Adjust the seasoning and serve, sprinkled with pepper and sesame oil.

Onion-Applesauce Soup

from Zuza
serves 4–6 people

The applesauce makes for a surprising flavor in this soup—you might call it the secret ingredient. It also serves to thicken the soup, so that the flour required in the French classic is not needed.

3	*large onions*
2 T	*butter*
1 T	*olive oil*
4	*cloves garlic, crushed*
1 t	*salt*
1½ t	*dried lemon thyme*
3 c	*dry white wine*
2 c	*applesauce, not too sweet*
3 c	*soup stock, and more as needed*
½ t	*Hungarian paprika*
	lemon juice, to taste
	black pepper, to taste

Quarter the onions lengthwise, then slice them thinly (also lengthwise). Heat the butter and oil in a heavy pot, add the onions and garlic along with the salt, and sauté for 20 minutes, stirring often so the onions do not brown. When they are soft, add the lemon thyme, wine, and apple sauce, and let simmer another 20 minutes.

Thin with stock if needed. Add the paprika, a splash of lemon juice, and pepper. Bring to a boil, turn off the heat, taste, and correct the seasoning.

This soup tastes wonderful with hot open-faced cheese sandwiches. It's also good with garlic croutons sprinkled on top or served on the side.

Carrot Surprise Soup

from Zuza
serves 4–6 people

This soup is a real hit, even with confirmed carrot-haters. Yes, there are actually people out there who despise this wonderful vegetable. Serve this soup to them . . . and to your best friends, your spouse's boss, or anybody you want to impress with your cooking. I have yet to meet anyone who can resist this soup. But make sure to buy carrots that have a strong taste—tender spring carrots don't have enough character to make this recipe work.

3 T	butter
2 c	yellow onion, chopped
¼ c	ginger root, grated
4	cloves garlic, coarsely chopped
1½ lb	carrots
4 c	dry white wine
4 c	orange juice
1 t	salt, or more to taste
	lemon juice, to taste
	black pepper, to taste
	a few drops of tabasco
¼ c	Italian parsley, finely chopped, plus some whole leaves for garnish

Heat the butter in the soup pot, add onions, ginger, and garlic, and sauté for 15 minutes or so. Do not let the onions brown. Meanwhile, peel and chop the carrots. Add them to the onions and sauté for several minutes.

Add the wine, bring to a boil, and let simmer for an hour, or until the carrots are very tender. Let cool. Puree in a food processor or with a hand blender. Put the puree back on the stove. Add as much orange juice as necessary to have the consistency you want. Bring to a boil, then turn off the heat.

Taste, and season with salt, lemon juice, pepper, and tabasco. Right before serving, stir in the parsley. Garnish in individual bowls with whole parsley leaves and orange slices.

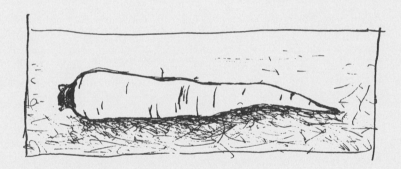

✦ CHAPTER 3 ✦

Salads

The salads presented here are quite varied, utilizing raw or cooked vegetables, grains, pasta, cheeses, nuts, fruit, and many kinds of dressings. So what makes a dish a salad?

In general, a salad is a creative combination of vegetables or fruits with other ingredients, eaten cold. Of course, as with most categorizations, this definition is imperfect—there are some salads it excludes, and some non-salads it would include (a smoothie is just *not* a salad). Nevertheless, it gives us a good basis for discussion and improvisation.

Green Salads

A salad, in its most basic form, is green lettuce—with something on top, called dressing. If the lettuce is fresh, and the dressing good, this could be all you need to satisfy your taste buds. The possibilities for improvisation upon this basic theme are unlimited. I'd like to leave it mostly to your imagination what those could be. But here are some suggestions and a few recipes to stimulate your creativity.

Explore the world of greens. Forego for awhile the ubiquitous iceberg lettuce, and try some other varieties. Romaine, green leaf, and red leaf lettuce all make a great base for a salad, but even they do not complete the palette available to you. There are also some spicy, bitterish greens like arugula (rocket), curly endive, Belgian endive, escarole, and watercress. These are usually too strong-tasting to make a salad of their own, but when mixed in moderate quantities with the milder greens, they make for a wonderful taste combination. Other possible additions include radicchio, spinach, sorrel, and finely shredded red or green cabbage—plus whole leaves of such herbs as basil, mint, and anise hyssop, or chopped fresh herbs such as dill, parsley, and anise or fennel stalks.

Use only fresh greens, and carefully sort out and discard any wilted ones. Separate the remaining leaves, wash them well, and dry them carefully. You can pat them dry with a clean dish towel, or invest in a salad spinner. The more water left on your greens, the less the taste of the dressing will come through; your salad will not only look soggy, but taste bland as well. When the leaves are dry, tear them into bite-sized pieces, and toss them with the other ingredients. If possible, do not refrigerate lettuce after washing it—but if you must do so, leave the leaves whole, and carefully wrap them in a dish towel.

Green salads are best made shortly before being eaten. Left to sit, they quickly lose their appeal. If, as a busy cook, you have to prepare a salad in advance, at least keep the greens separate from the other ingredients, especially the wet ones. Cover both the greens and the other ingredients with a cloth, and put them in a cool place. (Some non-green salads in fact require aging, such as marinated vegetable salad, potato salad, etc.)

Some people prefer to serve the dressing separately, but I think it is a good idea to toss the salad with *some* dressing, right before serving. Doing so will bind the flavors and establish the character of the salad, making it more than just the sum total of its ingredients. However, a dressed salad will not keep well for more than a few hours.

Possible ingredients for mixed salads include greens, tomato, cucumber, bell peppers, carrots, celery, corn, jicama, raw mushrooms, apples, pears, sections of citrus fruit and other tart fruit, plus:

- ✦ *toasted and chopped almonds*
- ✦ *toasted walnuts and blue cheese*

+ *toasted sunflower, sesame, or pumpkin seeds*
+ *cubes of marinated and baked or fried tofu, cold*
+ *chick peas and all kinds of beans, cooked and cooled*
+ *chopped anise and pineapple slices*
+ *hard boiled eggs*
+ *shredded cheddar, jack, Swiss, Feta, or any other cheese*
+ *pieces of Brie or goat cheese*

Another way to enrich a salad is to add a left-over or specially prepared batch of marinated or already dressed salad—such as carrot salad, marinated tomatoes, leeks in mustard vinaigrette, cucumber and kiwi in yogurt. I usually do not toss these dressed ingredients with the greens, but arrange them on top right before serving. This way the salad does not need an additional dressing.

The art of salad dressing is a whole separate subject in the world of gourmet cooking. It is well worth exploring, a fruitful ground for experiments and surprises in which "secret ingredients" really make the difference. Of course, it's fine to follow recipes—but if you stay with the spirit of creative experimentation, you will find a few tricks that will make your dressings taste like nobody else's.

The basic vinaigrette dressing for a green salad is made of one part vinegar and, depending on the strength of the vinegar, three or four parts olive oil, to which some salt, pepper, and a pinch of brown sugar are added, along with other herbs or spices when desired. Good vinegars to use are white wine, champagne, or tarragon vinegar. You can make the dressing in a glass jar with a tight-fitting lid; with the lid closed, shake for 10 seconds to mix the ingredients thoroughly. Many dressings will keep for days, so it's worthwhile to make extra for future use. Just be sure to taste an old dressing before you use it again—they seldom go bad, but their flavor may change over time.

There are also "white dressings," made with a base of yogurt, sour cream, mayonnaise, or buttermilk, to which are added herbs, spices, or strong-tasting cheeses (blue cheese or Feta in particular). These are easy to make and have the advantage of providing additional protein in the meal.

A few tips:

+ *Dark sesame oil is a nice variation on the oil theme*
+ *Various flavored vinegars will add an intriguing taste: raspberry, blueberry, balsamic, and sherry vinegar in particular*
+ *Fruit juices can replace lemon juice or part of it in a recipe*
+ *Pureed fruit such as bananas can be added to yogurt to make a light sweet-and-sour dressing*
+ *Blended herbs or greens make wonderful dressings: try watercress, arugula, or sorrel*
+ *Many dips or spreads can be thinned into salad dressings—tofu dips seem to be particularly suited for that purpose*
+ *Soy sauce, tahini, miso, umeboshi paste can be used to enhance the character of a dressing*
+ *Toasted sesame seeds lend a nutty flavor*
+ *Herbed or garlicky bread crumbs add crunchiness and flavor*

The Incredible
Tarragon–Mustard Vinaigrette

from Zuza
Makes 1¼ cups

An excellent dressing can elevate the simplest salad to unexpected heights. Here is a recipe for one such dressing which is suitable for a wide variety of mixed salads, especially when they are part of a Franco-Italian or other standard European menu.

1 T	*prepared Dijon mustard (the traditional mustard with seeds in it works very well here)*
2–3	*cloves garlic, pressed*
2 T	*fresh lemon juice*

¾ c	*olive oil*
	salt and pepper to taste
2 t	*dried tarragon or 2 T fresh, finely chopped*

In a small mixing bowl, stir the lemon juice and the garlic into the mustard with a fork, using a circular motion (not beating, but stirring). Slowly add the oil, stirring constantly and adding only as much at a time as you can incorporate with a few strokes of the fork. If you add too much, the dressing might curdle. What you are aiming for is a thick, mayonnaise-like consistency. When that's achieved, and you have used up all the oil, season with salt and pepper. Taste. If the mustard is overpowering, add a little more oil. If it tastes too oily, add lemon juice.

Add the tarragon last, and let the dressing stand while you prepare the salad. You can toss the salad with it or serve it on the side.

Here is an interesting variation of this dressing: omit the garlic, and add one egg yolk to the mustard, and, instead of tarragon, a cup of minced watercress leaves at the end. Exquisite!

I learned how to make this dressing from a portly fellow from St. Etienne, in my grape picking years in a small village in Provence. He emphasized the importance of a stirring, not a beating motion, and his dressings never curdled. Mine still do sometimes. I find it helps to have all the ingredients at room temperature. Also, you can save the dressing even when it's curdled by taking a small quantity of it, adding a teaspoon of mustard to this, then *very* slowly adding the rest of the curdled batch. By some subtle alchemy, it smoothes out again.

Mandarin Orange Salad

from Len Hilgerman
serves 4–6 people

1 head	lettuce, such as Boston, green leaf, or red leaf lettuce
1 head	Belgian endive
2 c	celery, diced
2 T	Italian parsley, finely chopped
6	green onions, white and green parts, finely chopped

The Dressing:

¼ c	tarragon vinegar
½ c	salad oil
½ t	salt
	several drops tabasco
2 T	brown sugar

The Topping:

2 cans	mandarin oranges
½ c	almonds, toasted in butter and slivered

Whisk the dressing ingredients together. Separate and wash the lettuce leaves, then spin or pat them dry. Tear into bite-size pieces. Mix the salad ingredients, and right before serving, toss with as much of the dressing as needed. Arrange the mandarin oranges on top. Sprinkle with almonds.

Spinach Salad
with Sesame Dressing

adapted from the *Odiyan Country Cookbook*, published by Dharma Publishing
serves 4–6 people

1	*bunch of fresh spinach*
8–10	*fresh firm mushrooms, sliced*
1	*medium ripe pear, cored and sliced*
12	*cherry tomatoes*
½	*small red onion, very thinly sliced*
2	*hard-boiled eggs, quartered lengthwise*

The Dressing:

¼ c	*vegetable oil*
3 T	*dark sesame oil*
4 T	*rice vinegar*
1 T	*grated fresh ginger root*
1 T	*tamari*
1 T	*honey*
¼ c	*toasted sesame seeds*

Combine the dressing ingredients, including the seeds. Wash the spinach, spin it dry and tear into bite-sized pieces. In a salad bowl, toss it with the other ingredients, reserving some of each, so that they can be arranged in a decorative pattern on top. Spoon some of the dressing (with the seeds) on top and serve the rest on the side.

Beet Salad with Eggs and Avocado

from Abbe Blum
serves 6–8 people

6	*medium beets*
6	*eggs*
3	*ripe but firm avocados*
3 T	*toasted walnuts*

The Dressing:

⅓ c	*mayonnaise*
⅓ c	*yogurt*
1 t	*black pepper*
2–3 T	*lime juice*
pinch	*ground cloves*
3 T	*fresh Italian parsley, finely chopped*

Scrub the beets, chop off the rough ends, and boil until tender. Let them cool, then peel and cube them into ½" chunks.

Boil the eggs, and quarter them lengthwise. Cut the avocados into thin wedges.

Whisk the dressing ingredients together, and pour into a small bowl or pitcher.

Arrange the salad ingredients artistically on a white platter, without mixing them. Sprinkle with walnuts. Spoon only a small amount of dressing on the salad, so as not to blur the design, and serve the rest on the side.

Cucumber and Feta Salad

from Zuza
serves 4–6 people

The Dressing:

3 T	olive oil
2 T	white wine vinegar
1 T	fresh mint, finely chopped
	salt and pepper, to taste
pinch	brown sugar
	a few drops of tabasco

The Salad:

3	cucumbers
1	bunch of scallions, chopped
½ c	crumbled Feta cheese

Whisk the dressing ingredients together. Remember that feta cheese is usually very salty, so use salt sparingly. Peel and thinly slice the cucumber. Add dressing and scallions. Sprinkle with Feta right before serving.

If you make this salad in advance, refrigerate it, and when you are ready to serve it, drain excess liquid before adding the cheese. Reserve the liquid to add to another salad dressing—it is especially good mixed with yogurt or used to thin mayonnaise.

Salade en Brochettes

from Zuza
Makes about 12 skewers

An unusual presentation of marinated vegetables. The vegetables are sliced and steamed until barely tender, and then allowed to soak in the marinade for a long time before they are skewered. The result is delicious and pleasing to the eye, a good addition to an elegant buffet menu.

2	*medium carrots, sliced ½" thick*
2	*medium zucchini, sliced ½" thick*
4	*large kohlrabis, sliced ½" thick, the slices then cut in quarters*
16	*medium mushrooms, cleaned, stems removed*
16	*cherry tomatoes*
16	*pearl onions, peeled*

The Marinade:

⅓ c	*olive oil*
½ c	*balsamic vinegar*
1 T	*dried herbs or 3 T fresh: a mixture of basil, oregano, savory, marjoram (not too much—very strong taste), thyme, rosemary*
½ t	*salt*
½ t	*black pepper*
	a few drops tabasco

Steam the zucchini, carrots, and kohlrabi until barely tender. Toss all the vegetables with the marinade, and let sit at least overnight and as long as a few days. Stir occasionally. Skewer before serving, mixing the vegetables for a colorful presentation.

These are also excellent broiled.

Leeks in Tarragon and Mustard Vinaigrette

from Zuza
serves 4–6 people

3–4	*leeks, white parts only*

N *ote:* There is more to the "white parts" than meets the eye. When you cut off the green part of a leek and discard only a few outer leaves, very often you will find underneath some more partly white (or pale green) leaves, which also can be included in this recipe. Cut off *their* green part, and look for more white "surprises" inside.

The Dressing:

1 T	*prepared Dijon mustard*
2–3	*cloves garlic, pressed*
2 T	*fresh lemon juice*
¾ c	*olive oil*
	salt and pepper to taste
2 t	*dried tarragon or 2 T fresh, finely chopped*

C ut the leeks in half lengthwise, then in 1" thick slices on the diagonal. In a colander, rinse them under cold running water. Be sure to rinse all the sand from between the leaves. It is okay for the leaves to separate.

Steam them 15–20 minutes, or until they are tender and have lost their "bite"; then let them cool slightly. Meanwhile prepare the dressing (its recipe is in the introduction to this chapter). While the leeks are still warm, toss them with enough dressing to coat them well. Let them stand a few hours. If refrigerated, bring to room temperature before serving.

Tomatoes To Swoon For

from Frances Strassman
serves 4 people

3	*medium organic beefsteak tomatoes*
½	*small red onion, minced*
1½ T	*balsamic vinegar*
	minced garlic, finely chopped or whole (optional)
	fresh basil leaves, finely chopped or whole (optional)

S lice the tomatoes about ⅓ inch thick. Place them on a serving dish, and sprinkle the onion over them. Then drizzle vinegar onto each slice, and put them in the refrigerator to marinate for 15 to 30 minutes.

You can add garlic and basil to the vinegar to intensify its flavor. Or layer the tomato slices alternately with whole basil leaves on a nice platter, then sprinkle with onion and vinegar.

Polish Holiday Vegetable Salad

from Zuza
serves 10–12 people

This medley of cooked, diced veggies was a favorite dish when I was growing up in Poland. It was often served at holidays, when many relatives gathered together.

5	potatoes
7	medium carrots, peeled
2½ c	pinto or small white or red beans (1 c dry), or 3 c green peas (could be canned)
1	medium white onion, uncooked
6	eggs
3	Granny Smith apples, uncooked
4	dill pickles
3 c	mushrooms, sliced
1 c	red wine vinegar
	a few corns of allspice
2	bay leaves
2	whole cloves
1 T	salt
1 T	pepper
2 T	Dijon mustard
¾ c	mayonnaise
	apple cider vinegar

There are several steps to do the day before, including some pre-cooking to help several ingredients hold their shape when diced. Hard boil the eggs. Also boil the potatoes in their skins—with the eggs, if you like. Peel and steam the carrots. If you are using dried beans, soak them in cold water. And marinate the mushrooms in a glass jar with the heated red wine vinegar, allspice, bay leaves, and cloves—one teaspoon of pickling spices could be mixed with the hot vinegar instead.

On the day the salad will be served, boil the beans, drain them, and let them come to room temperature. Peel the eggs and potatoes. Drain the mushrooms, discarding the spices. Dice the potatoes, carrots, eggs, mushrooms, apples, onion, and pickles to green pea size. Gently mix them all together with the beans (or green peas), salt, pepper, and mustard, adding the eggs at the very last so they will maintain their shape.

Let the combination sit for 3 hours in the refrigerator. Just before serving, add the mayonnaise, plus a splash of apple cider vinegar to enhance the flavor, and taste for spices. I recommend serving this dish with a heavy, dark rye bread, a light soup, and a green salad.

Exotic Black Bean and Fruit Salad

from Abbe Blum
serves 4–6 people

The earthy beans and tangy fruit make an unexpected and refreshing combination. This salad is great with Polenta Supreme.

1½ c	dried black beans
3	small cloves garlic, chopped
1	large clove garlic, minced
3 T	fresh lime juice
3 c	mango, chopped (2–3 mangoes)
1 c	fresh pineapple, chopped finely
⅛ t	hot red pepper flakes
¼ c	fresh cilantro, chopped
½ t	salt, to taste

Clean and rinse the beans, then soak them overnight in cold water. The next day, drain and rinse them; then put them in a saucepan with the onion and chopped garlic. Cover these with 3 cups of cold water. Simmer over medium heat until tender but firm (30 to 40 minutes). Drain them; then rinse them in cold water until they are cool.

Add all the other ingredients to the cooked beans, tossing them until they are thoroughly mixed. Let the salad sit to allow the flavors to marry.

Marinated Veggie Salad

from Zuza
serves 4–6 people

1 c	carrots, diced, lightly steamed
1 c	green beans, cut in small pieces and lightly steamed
1 c	cauliflower, divided into very small florets, lightly steamed
1 c	corn, boiled
1 c	cooked kidney beans
1 c	mushrooms, quartered
1 c	cherry tomatoes, halved
1	medium red onion, finely diced

The Marinade:

¾ c	balsamic vinegar
½ c	olive oil
1 ½ T	dried herbs or 4 T fresh: a mixture of basil, oregano, savory, marjoram (not too much—the taste is strong), thyme, rosemary
½ t	salt
½ t	black pepper
	a few drops tabasco

Toss the vegetables with the marinade, and refrigerate at least overnight and as long as a few days. Stir occasionally. Before serving, bring the mixture to room temperature, taste, and adjust seasoning. You might want to drain the salad before serving, since the marinade can be reserved and used again within a few weeks. Serve as an antipasto, garnished with fresh herbs, hard-boiled eggs, and tomato wedges.

Lentil Salad

from Abbe Blum
serves 8–10 people

This salad is easy to make, but it needs some aging. It is best when prepared at least one day in advance.

1 lb	dried lentils
1 c	currants
1 c	red onions, finely chopped
⅓ c	capers (optional)
¼ c	chopped almonds, roasted
2	red bell peppers
	olive oil for the peppers

The Marinade:

¾ c	vegetable oil
½ c	red wine vinegar
2 T	brown sugar
1 t	cumin
1 t	dry mustard
1 t	cinnamon
½ t	mace
½ t	coriander
1 t	cardamom
½ t	ground cloves
½ t	nutmeg
2 t	salt
1 t	pepper
dash	cayenne

W hisk the marinade ingredients together. Rinse the lentils, boil until just tender, then drain them well. While still warm, toss them with the marinade. Refrigerate overnight.

Preheat oven to 400°. Cut peppers in half lengthwise, take out seeds and veins, and lightly brush both sides with olive oil. Bake with skin side up on a tray until the skins are wrinkled and have slightly changed color. Cool, scrape off skin, and slice peppers into ½" x 1" strips.

Two hours before serving, remove them from the refrigerator, and stir in the onions, capers, tangerine segments, and almonds. Let them sit at room temperature until serving.

Tortellini Salad

from Zuza
serves 4–6 people

1 lb	tortellini, fresh or dry
1	large red pepper, diced
1	large green pepper, diced
1	large yellow pepper, diced
3	stalks of celery, chopped
1	small bunch of Italian parsley, chopped
6	Roma tomatoes, cut in wedges
½ c	mayonnaise, or more (can be replaced in part by yogurt)
2	cloves of garlic
	salt and pepper, to taste
	lemon juice, to taste
pinch	cayenne

Boil the tortellini according to package directions. Drain, and toss with the peppers, celery, and parsley. ·

Press the garlic into the mayonnaise. Add to the salad. Season with salt, pepper, lemon juice, and cayenne. You might want to add more mayonnaise if the salad seems too dry.

Let stand an hour before serving to allow the flavors to marry.

Fred's Mango Salad

from Fred Lippman
serves 10–12 people

This is a molded salad with a pale yellow color and a bright, surprising taste. It looks like a dessert, but it isn't. Serve as you would cranberry sauce. This salad will serve to set off softer, sweeter flavors of the other dishes on your menu.

3 pkg	lemon flavored Jello (3 oz each)
2 c	boiling water
2	15 oz cans mangoes, drained (juice reserved)
8 oz	cream cheese, room temperature, cut in pieces
1	kiwi, peeled and sliced for garnish

Combine the Jello and water in a large bowl, and stir until dissolved. Let cool. Add the mango juice. Combine the canned mangoes and cream cheese in a blender, and mix until creamy. Blend this into the gelatin mixture. Lightly brush a 6 cup round mold (a bundt cake pan works well) with mayonnaise. Pour the gelatin mixture into the mold, and refrigerate until set. When it is ready, place the mold for 10 seconds in a larger bowl filled with hot water. The salad should then separate easily from the mold. Turn onto a plate, and decorate with kiwi slices.

Moroccan Confetti Salad

from Zuza
serves 4–6 people

The Dressing:

½ c	vegetable oil
	juice of 2 lemons, or more to taste
½ t	cinnamon
¼ t	ground cloves
½ c	fresh orange juice
⅛ t	cayenne
2 t	fresh mint leaves, chopped
4 T	fresh Italian parsley, chopped
½ c	currants

Begin by whisking together the dressing ingredients; then add the currants. The dressing will develop its flavor while you prepare the rest of the salad, and the currants will soak up some of the dressing's concentrated goodness.

The Salad:

2 c	dry couscous
1 t	salt
1 ½ c	apple juice
1 c	diced carrots
1	package frozen green peas
1	red bell pepper, diced
1	yellow bell pepper, diced
1	jicama, diced
½	bunch green onions, chopped (white and green parts)
	toasted, chopped almonds (optional)

The success of this dish depends partly on the kind of couscous you use and on sensing just how much liquid and time it needs to become tender without getting mushy. It took me a few failed experiments to figure out my method; I use instant couscous that does not require cooking. If you can find it in your store, proceed as follows:

Place the couscous and salt in a bowl or pot that can be covered with a tight fitting lid. Boil the apple juice. Pour it immediately over the couscous, stir once with a slotted spoon, cover and let sit for a few minutes . . . but not too long. You want to catch the moment when the grains are already tender. At that moment it is essential to uncover the pot and fluff the grain with a fork, so that all the steam is let out and the couscous does not get a chance to cook further and become a solid block of mush.

If you get a different type of couscous, follow the directions on the package, and be prepared for surprises. What you want to achieve is grains that do not stick together too much, and are no longer hard or raw tasting. *Note:* If you double the amount of couscous, *don't* double that of the apple juice. Remember that the more grain you cook, the smaller the *proportional* amount of liquid needed. For example, if you use 4 cups of couscous, use 3½ cups apple juice.

The rest of the preparation is simple. Steam the chopped carrots and the peas separately until barely tender. Add them to the cooked couscous along with the peppers, jicama, and onions. Toss this mixture with the dressing. It is best to let this salad sit a few hours to allow the flavors to blend.

Before serving, sprinkle the almonds on top if you wish. They add a crunchy texture and make the salad sweeter.

Carrot Salads

Grated carrots make wonderful salads. Their taste varies depending on the other ingredients and dressing used. Usually these salads improve over time—plan ahead so the flavor will have time to develop. I always make a large quantity so there will be some left over for the next day; because carrot salads mix well with other salad makings, "leftovers" easily become new dishes.

Some people say it's enough to scrub carrots well before grating them. I recommend thinly peeling them instead, because the skins are often bitter. The exception would be young, tender carrots of the new season; their peel is just as sweet as their inside.

Sweet-and-Sour Carrot Salad

from Zuza
serves 4–6 people

5	*medium carrots, grated*
3	*green, tart apples, cored (but not peeled), grated*
	handful of dried prunes, chopped and soaked in a cup of Marsala

The Dressing:

3 T	*light vegetable oil*
	juice of one lemon

Mix the carrots, apples, prunes, and Marsala. Toss them with the oil and lemon juice. Or omit the prunes, and add a few tablespoons of finely chopped fresh mint instead.

Carrot Salad with a Hint of the Orient

from Zuza
serves 4–6 people

5	medium carrots, grated
3 T	sesame seeds, toasted

The Dressing:

6 T	light vegetable oil
2 t	honey
4 T	lemon juice
2 T	rice vinegar
2 t	grated fresh ginger

Mix all the dressing ingredients well, toss with the carrots, and sprinkle the sesame seeds on top.

Carrots with Tarragon-Mustard Dressing

from Zuza
serves 4–6 people

6	large carrots
⅓ c	coarsely chopped walnuts
1 T	walnut oil (optional)

The Dressing:

1 T	prepared Dijon mustard
	juice of 1–2 lemons
¾ c	olive oil
	salt and pepper to taste
2 t	dried tarragon—or 2 T fresh, finely chopped

Prepare the dressing according to the recipe in the introduction to this chapter, omitting the garlic. This dressing should taste quite strong and sharp—the carrots will absorb a lot of the heat. Toss the carrots with the dressing, and let them sit for up to two hours.

Toast the walnuts lightly; putting them in the oven at 300° for a few minutes works well. You can also use a skillet on a low flame, but stir often and watch closely, since the walnuts will burn easily if you turn your back on them. You can add some walnut oil while they are toasting. Once they have cooled, chop the walnuts, and sprinkle them on top of the carrots just before serving.

Summer Cole Slaw

from Frances Strassman
serves 4 people

½ c	plain nonfat yogurt
1 t	honey (optional)
½ c	shredded carrot
¼ c	celery, minced
2 T	fresh cilantro, minced
1 c	red cabbage, chopped
1 c	green cabbage, chopped
¼ c	green pepper, minced
1–2	cloves garlic, crushed
1 T	your favorite vinegar

Mix the yogurt, honey, vinegar, and cilantro. Add the vegetables. Marinate at least ½ hour. Toss again before serving.

✦ CHAPTER 4 ✦

Entrées

Menu-making for a vegetarian meal is very different from planning for a steak-and-potato dinner. The category of "entrées" does exist in the vegetarian cuisine, but a vegetarian entrée does not play the same dominant role as, for example, the classic pot roast. I often wonder whether it makes any sense to distinguish one part of a vegetarian meal as the "main dish."

Vegetarian cooking is more a matter of combining different types of dishes in the same meal. A good illustration of this principle is a classic Indian dinner. Consider the array of different curries, rice, a bowl of lentil soup, and a bowl of yogurt, all served on one large platter with at least one kind of bread. There is really no main dish. Instead, the different elements complement one another to produce a magnificent whole.

This section presents recipes for some dishes that may be regarded as the central feature of a meal, though most will not make a meal by themselves. Suggestions are usually offered as to what could be served with them, but there are no set rules. Everything depends on the cook's willingness to use his or her imagination and sensitivity—and to experiment.

Planning a menu is always an adventure that involves stepping into an unknown territory with curiosity and openness. As usual, the unknown is both exciting and a little scary, since a successful outcome is up to you!

Here is an impasse often met in menu planning. Something begins to emerge—say, you think of one dish you would like to serve. But you get attached to that item, perhaps a sweet potato salad, and try as you may, nothing else that comes to mind fits with it—asparagus is too starchy, a carrot soup too orange, and so on. In such a case, it is often helpful to let go of that favorite idea and start anew. The end of the process is a wonderful surprise: everything suddenly falls into place, and an entirely satisfying menu comes together.

As you exercise your creativity, I suggest you look to this fundamental principle for wholesome guidance both in vegetarian cooking and in the rest of life: *balance.*

In vegetarian meals, nutritional balance is especially important, since meat, one obvious source of protein, is removed from the table. In the recipes presented here, cheese and other dairy products are often used to provide protein (as well as wonderful flavors), as are other foods, including tofu, beans, soy milk, nuts, and whole grains. If the "main dish" contains no protein, be sure to include some in the other parts of the meal. That could mean a fortified grain dish, a yogurt salad dressing, or a low fat cheese dessert.

Balance applies to taste as well as to nutrition. Let sweet play with sour; let spicy hot be offset by cool; and let assertive flavors emerge among more neutral tastes. Contrast the textures, too: when one dish is crunchy, make another soft and smooth; when one is heavy, the rest should be light. When a dish is set off from another in this way, their flavors and textures will complement each other.

Visual presentation is part of the meal, too. If you make a simple meal look like a feast, it will taste more like one. Use flowers or whole herb leaves as garnish, and arrange the salad ingredients in fanciful patterns. You can use the shapes, textures, and colors of the different vegetables and dishes to compose a work of art.

Monochromatic meals are worth occasional consideration for aesthetic reasons. You might combine, for example, beet soup and a red cabbage salad with a purple plum dessert, or a carrot curry with saffron rice and a mandarin orange salad. But use such a limited palette only once in a while; many like-colored foods have similar nutrition content, so variety is healthier.

On Cutting the Onions

The majority of the following recipes require chopped onions, which might be a problem for people with sensitive eyes.

There are many excellent ways of avoiding tears while cutting onions. However, I have found all of them to be inefficient under certain psychological circumstances. If I approach an onion with the heart of a fearless warrior, it cannot get to me. But when I am cranky, lazy, or generally resistant to cooking, my eyes sting, burn, and water like fountains as soon as I begin even peeling one.

Here is the advice I have received:

✦ *Rinse the peeled onions in warm water before cutting*

✦ *Keep them in the freezer for a few hours before handling them*

✦ *Do the chopping near an open window*

✦ *Soak the knife in lemon juice*

✦ *Put a piece of onion on your head (this tip is from the book* Like Water for Chocolate)

✦ *Before you begin the job, take a piece of commercial, sliced bread, put it over your face, and deeply inhale through it a few times*

✦ *Stick your tongue out while chopping*

✦ Never *solve this problem by chopping onions in a food processor—they are apt to turn into a bitter mush*

Finally, you can always think of something in your life that could use a little grieving, and combine two useful activities. By the time the onions are chopped, your sadness is released, and you can prepare the rest of the meal in a calm and joyful state of mind.

By the way, many recipes start with: "Chop one medium onion," and this little phrase is often enough to set me on automatic pilot. Absent-mindedly, I do whatever I usually do to chop an onion, forgetting that this experience could be as fresh and alive as it was when I first learned to cook. So the next time you face an onion, ask yourself: In how many shapes and ways could I cut it? Then go ahead, chop one medium onion as you never have before. And enjoy the rest of the meal preparation, as well.

Tofu, Mushroom, and Olive Scramble

from Joyce McCann
serves 4–6 people

Once Joyce planned an omelet for a retreat breakfast—then discovered we were out of eggs. This dish was her solution. It proved so delicious that we served it at our first Sunday Gourmet Brunch.

4 T	butter
½	bunch of scallions (10 scallions or so), chopped
2	packages tofu (we use semi-firm, but any kind should be okay)
6 c	fresh mushrooms, very finely minced (can be done in a food processor)
1 c	black olives, pitted and minced
¼ c	Italian parsley
	salt and pepper to taste

Melt 2 tablespoons of the butter in a large skillet, add the scallions, and sauté over a medium flame until soft. Add the tofu, and mash with a fork. Heat for about 7–8 minutes, or until the tofu is completely dry. Transfer to a bowl.

In the same skillet, without adding butter, fry the mushrooms until they release their juice and then let all the liquid evaporate. The mushrooms will change their color in the process.

Return the tofu to the skillet. Add the olives, parsley, and remaining 2 tablespoons of butter. Season with salt and pepper. Heat through before serving.

Potato and Smoked Gouda Casserole

from Zuza
serves 6 people

S erved with a crisp green salad and fruit for dessert, this excellent dish reflects the days when nobody believed that good things could be bad for you.

1	*large yellow onion*
2 c	*sour cream*
2 c	*grated mozzarella*
2 c	*Dutch smoked Gouda or other smoked cheese*
6	*large potatoes*
1½ t	*salt*
2 T	*paprika*
	pepper to taste
⅓ c	*wheat germ or dry bread crumbs*

C hop the onion, and mix it with the sour cream. Add the cheeses. Oil a 9" x 13" glass casserole. Preheat the oven to 350°.

Peel and thinly slice the potatoes. Arrange half of them in the casserole, sprinkling them with 1½ teaspoons salt, 1 tablespoon paprika, and some freshly ground black pepper. Spread half of the sour cream mixture on top.

Repeat the layers, including the spices. The sour cream mixture should be the last layer.

Sprinkle with bread crumbs. Cover with foil. Bake for about two hours at 350°.

Oven Roasted Vegetables

from Zuza
serves 4–6 people

This is a great way to serve even the simplest vegetables. Roast the vegetables in separate pans, since they cook at different speeds—but you can serve them artistically arranged on one large platter. The beautiful colors and shapes allow you to create a delightful composition as the centerpiece for your dinner table. Use any combination of vegetables for a fancy menu—or just one kind, for a simple and delicious side dish.

Vegetables (in order of the length of cooking time):	Recommended herbs (dried):
small new potatoes	lemon thyme
carrots	tarragon
eggplant	basil
zucchini	marjoram
shallots, or small pearl onions	rosemary
kohlrabi	dill
peppers	basil
cherry tomatoes	oregano
vegetables of your choice	olive oil, coarse sea salt, several garlic cloves, thinly slivered

Preheat the oven to 350°. Wash and trim the vegetables, and cut them in your favorite shapes. Keep the different vegetables separate. In a big mixing bowl, toss each batch with a little olive oil, so that as many pieces as possible get coated with a thin film of oil. Arrange each group in a shallow baking dish, and sprinkle with herbs and salt. Use only coarse salt—it has the magic property of drawing water out of vegetables, making their taste more concentrated.

Add a lot of garlic with the eggplant and zucchini. You can make little slits in the vegetable slices with a sharp pointed knife and actually stuff them with the garlic.

Place the baking dishes in the oven, and remove each when its vegetables are tender. Carrots take about 50 minutes, zucchinis half an hour, tomatoes only 10 minutes or so. Often I cover the pans with aluminum foil, which seems to speed up the process without ruining the effect.

Potatoes have played so many tricks on me that I do not feel up to making any predictions regarding their cooking time. However, since these vegetables are great served at room temperature, timing is not critical in this recipe.

It is best to make this recipe when you have other things to do in the kitchen anyway and are not in a big hurry.

Asparagus and Mushroom Pie

from Zuza
serves 4–6 people

The Potato Crust:

3	*large raw potatoes*
1 t	*salt*
2	*large eggs, beaten*

The Topping:

4	*large cloves garlic*
1	*bunch green onions*
2	*bunches asparagus*
15	*medium-size mushrooms*
3 T	*butter*
½ t	*salt*
½ t	*dried basil*
dash	*thyme*
2½ c	*white cheddar cheese, grated*
2	*large eggs*
¼ c	*milk*

Preheat the oven to 400°. To make the crust, peel and grate the potatoes, combine with salt, and turn into a colander. Let drain 10 minutes, then squeeze out excess moisture. Transfer to a bowl, and combine with the eggs. Pat into an oiled 9" x 13" baking dish to make a crust. Bake in preheated oven 35–40 minutes.

Meanwhile, peel and crush the garlic, and chop the onion, asparagus tips, and mushrooms. Sauté the onions and garlic in butter for a few minutes. Add the asparagus and mushrooms along with the seasonings. If the mixture is still very moist, use a slotted spoon to avoid getting too much liquid into the pie. Cover, and cook for 5–7 minutes, stirring occasionally. Then uncover, cooking for a few minutes more to reduce the juices.

Take the crust out of the oven, and turn the temperature down to 375°. Spread half the cheese on the baked crust. On top of this, spread the vegetable sauté. Cover with the remaining cheese. Beat the eggs with milk, and pour over the pie. Bake 35–40 minutes at 375°.

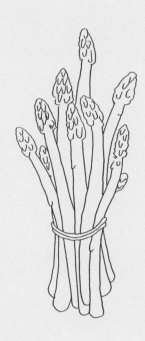

Mediterranean Stew

from Zuza
serves 4–6 people

A dish of subtle fragrance and exciting flavor. It requires a substantial amount of preparation, but it is well worth the effort.

3 T	olive oil
2	large onions, chopped
5	cloves garlic, crushed
2 t	ground cumin
1 t	turmeric
½ t	ground cloves
½ t	cinnamon
2	dried hot peppers, crushed
1 t	paprika
1 c	carrots, sliced
2 c	sweet potatoes, cubed
4 c	eggplant, cubed
2 c	zucchini, sliced
1	green pepper, sliced
1	red pepper, sliced
4	large tomatoes, diced
½ c	fresh cilantro leaves, chopped
1 c	garbanzo beans, boiled until barely tender
½ c	dried currants
2 c	orange juice
¼ c	lemon juice
	fresh Italian parsley, chopped
	toasted chopped almonds

Sauté the onions in oil until translucent. Stir in the garlic and spices (including the hot peppers), and after two minutes, the carrots and sweet potatoes. Continue sautéing, gradually adding the eggplant, zucchini, and peppers. Let them simmer for a few minutes before you add the tomatoes, cilantro, garbanzo beans, and currants.

Pour the orange juice over the stew, cover, and let simmer for 15–20 minutes, until all the vegetables are tender. Just before serving, add the lemon juice and adjust the seasoning. Garnish with parsley and almonds. Serve with couscous, Cucumber and Feta Salad, and Grapes in Lemon Yogurt.

Seaweed Stew
with Shiitake and Spinach

from Zuza
serves 4–6 people

2 T	sesame oil
3	cloves garlic, minced
12	shiitake mushrooms, dried or fresh
2 c	daikon, sliced in half-moons
4 c	zucchini, sliced in half-moons
12 oz	wakame seaweed, soaked briefly in cold water and coarsely chopped
	freshly ground black pepper, to taste
¼ c	tamari soy sauce or more, to taste
2	bunches fresh spinach (with stems), washed and coarsely chopped
½ c	toasted sunflower seeds

If you are using dried mushrooms, soak them in a small amount of hot water at least half an hour in advance. If you are using fresh mushrooms, wash them and trim off any parts that don't look fresh. Cut them into thin slivers.

Heat the oil in a heavy skillet, add the garlic, and stir-fry it for a minute over a medium-high flame. Add the mushrooms. Sauté for a few minutes. Add the daikon and zucchini and sauté until their color deepens—they are best when still a little crunchy, so do not overcook them. Add the wakame, and let it simmer for 5 more minutes. Season with pepper and soy sauce.

Add the spinach, and cook briefly only until it has wilted. Adjust seasoning. Serve immediately, sprinkled with toasted sunflower seeds.

Spinach Pasta with Roquefort and Walnuts

from Zuza
serves 4–6 people

1 lb	spinach fettucine
1 t	salt
2 T	olive oil
1 c	crumbled Roquefort cheese (or Gorgonzola)
½ c	toasted walnuts, coarsely chopped
4 T	olive oil
4 T	finely chopped fresh basil leaves

Boil the pasta in 6 quarts of water with salt and olive oil. In the serving boil, mix together the cheese, nuts and basil. Add the pasta when it is done, toss well. Then add the olive oil and stir once more. Serve immediately.

Sun-Dried Tomato Pasta

from Zuza
serves 4–6 people

Many people find the taste of sun-dried tomatoes quite addictive, so if you have not encountered them before, be warned. They are the highlight of this dish, their flavor enhanced by lemon zest and garlic.

8 oz	sun-dried tomatoes
1 c	fresh basil leaves
½ c	grated lemon zest
4	cloves garlic
½ c	olive oil
1 t	salt
2 t	coarsely ground black pepper
¾ c	black olives, preferably Greek or French, pitted and sliced
1 lb	dried pasta (spinach linguini or similar kind)
¾ c	crumbled feta cheese

If you are using tomatoes packed in oil, drain them well. Save the oil to substitute for part of the olive oil in this recipe. If you are using dry tomatoes, soak them in a small amount of hot water for at least half an hour (the liquid can also be added to the sauce).

In the food processor, blend the basil, lemon zest, and garlic with the olive oil, salt, and pepper. At the end, add the tomatoes and process briefly, so the sauce is still chunky. Work with a spatula, turning the processor on for a few seconds at a time, and scraping the sides of the bowl in between. Be sure not to overprocess into a mushy paste. Add a little hot water (or a little of the liquid in which the tomatoes were soaking) if the sauce is too thick.

Transfer to a mixing bowl. Stir in the olives, cover, and let stand at room temperature for a few hours. At serving time, boil the pasta, toss with the sauce, sprinkle the feta cheese on top—and get ready for a culinary experience that you will want to repeat over and over again.

Sesame Noodles with Roasted Eggplant

from Zuza
serves 4–6 people

As with all dishes that contain acidic marinades, use glass, ceramic, or stainless steel mixing bowls to prepare and to store this salad. In the unlikely case that there is some left over, it does keep well for several days.

1	*large eggplant*
2	*cloves garlic*

The Marinade:

½ c	*dark sesame oil*
½ c	*soy sauce*
¼ c	*balsamic vinegar*
3 T	*brown sugar*
½ t	*salt*
1 t	*hot chili oil*
1	*bunch of scallions*
¼ c	*chopped cilantro, plus a few whole leaves for garnish*
3	*cloves garlic, pressed*
2 T	*freshly grated ginger root*
1	*12 oz package Japanese soba noodles*
⅓ c	*toasted sesame seeds*

Preheat the oven to 375°. Cut the eggplant in half lengthwise, and place the pieces flat side up in an oiled baking dish. Peel the garlic, slice it thinly, and stuff it into the eggplant flesh. Brush the eggplant with olive oil. Bake uncovered at 375° for 45 minutes, or until the eggplant is soft but not mushy.

Whisk together all of the marinade ingredients, *except* the ginger and garlic. Boil the noodles according to package directions—*al dente*, not too soft. Divide the marinade in two. Pour one half of it over the noodles, and toss well.

Add the ginger and garlic to the other half of the marinade. When the eggplant is done and is cool enough to handle, peel it and cut or tear it into narrow strips. Place the strips in the ginger-and-garlic marinade so they are entirely covered.

For best results, the two main parts of the salad should now be covered and refrigerated, overnight if possible. Two hours before serving, combine them. Add the sesame seeds, and garnish with whole cilantro leaves.

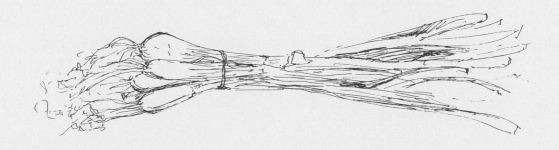

Pasta with Eggplant Sauce

from Dave Davis
serves 4–6 people

This dish is best with shells or other forms of pasta that can catch and hold its thick sauce.

2	*eggplants*
¼ c	*olive oil, plus some for brushing*
½ c	*Kalamata olives, drained and rinsed*
3 T	*capers, drained and rinsed*
½ t	*red pepper flakes*
⅓ c	*fresh basil, chopped*
⅓ c	*fresh Italian parsley, chopped*
6	*stalks celery, cut thinly lengthwise, then diced*
1	*large onion, diced*
6-8	*cloves garlic, minced*
2 T	*red wine vinegar*
32 oz	*canned tomatoes, chopped, with their juice*
½ c	*currants*
1 lb	*pasta shells*
1 c	*crumbled feta*

Cut the eggplants into half-inch slices. Brush the slices with olive oil and bake in a hot (425°) oven, turning once, to quickly brown them on both sides. (A broiler works well.) When the eggplants are ready, take them out of the oven. Let them cool, and cut them in half-inch chunks.

Mix together the herbs, olives, capers, and red pepper flakes.

Heat ¼ cup olive oil in a heavy skillet, and fry the celery over medium heat. When it starts to brown, turn the heat to low and add the onion, garlic, and salt. Sauté 5–7 minutes, until soft. Add the vinegar, and turn the heat to high. Stir in the herb and olive mixture. Add the eggplant, currants, and tomatoes. Stir, and bring the sauce to a boil. Then reduce the heat, and let simmer for about 15 minutes.

Cook the pasta *al dente.* Drain and toss well with the sauce. Add the feta, and toss again. Serve immediately.

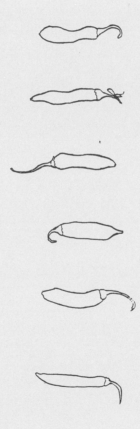

Sauerkraut Delight

from Zuza
serves 4–6 people

This is a vegetarian version of the traditional Polish hunters' stew, *bigos*. Being vegetarian, it is completely different from the original dish and many times lower in fat, which would disqualify it for a Polish hunter— but I think you'll enjoy it. Incidentally, if you are one of those people who can't stand sauerkraut, try this recipe anyway—it bears very little resemblance to sauerkraut as it is usually prepared in this country.

4 T	oil
2	large onions, coarsely chopped
1 t	salt
1	can (32 oz) sauerkraut
1	medium head white cabbage, shredded
	handful of chopped dried prunes
1 c	dry white wine
1 t	ground cloves
½ t	ground allspice
½ t	cinnamon
	a pinch of cayenne

Take the sauerkraut out of the can, put it into a colander, and lightly squeeze to eliminate excess liquid. The liquid tends to be very salty, but it also contains minerals and vitamins, so leave some in. In a medium skillet, sauté one of the onions with 2 tablespoons oil. When the onion begins to turn a deep gold (which may take as long as 15 minutes), add the sauerkraut and sauté for another 10–15 minutes.

Meanwhile, in a heavy pot, sauté the other onion with 2 tablespoons of oil and 1 teaspoon of salt until translucent. Add the shredded cabbage, and sauté for 5–7 minutes, until wilted. You can add the cabbage by handfuls; it will shrink as it cooks.

Transfer the sauerkraut into the cabbage pot; add the wine, spices, and prunes. Let it simmer over a low flame for an hour or longer, depending on your preference. A shorter cooking time will yield a crunchier texture, while a longer time will make a sweeter taste and a more enticing blend of flavors.

Adjust the seasonings before serving. If it's too sour, add a little honey. Serve with boiled whole potatoes and Herbed Cheese Spread.

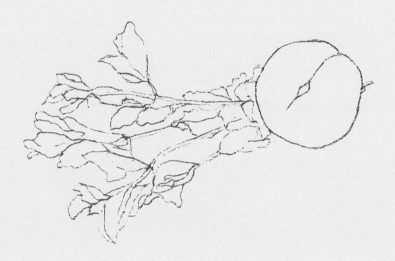

Crisp Fried Marinated Tofu

from Bill Farthing
serves 4–6 people

Easily prepared, this tofu makes a flavorful appetizer or adds something special to a stir-fry. Start preparation about 2 hours before you plan to serve it.

1 lb	*block of firm tofu*
½ c	*soy sauce*
1 T	*onion, finely diced*
2 t	*garlic, finely diced*
2 t	*fresh ginger, peeled and grated*
¼ c	*cornstarch (approx.)*
	oil for deep frying

Drain the tofu and press it firmly. Then cube it. The cubing technique pictured here makes uniform pieces and is simple to do. First cut the block horizontally into two slabs. Next, keeping the two slabs together, make the remaining cuts: two along the length, and three along the width.

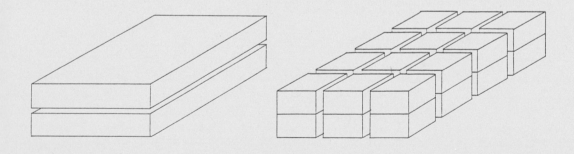

Select a bowl slightly larger than needed to hold the tofu. In it, prepare the marinade by mixing the spices into the soy sauce; dried spices may be used, but decrease the quantities by half. Add the tofu.

Marinate for at least an hour, turning a few times. Stirring the cubes may damage them, so use a rubber spatula.

Drain the tofu, saving the marinade. Place the tofu on a platter, and dust it with the cornstarch until each cube is completely coated. Deep fry until golden brown. Serve soon, using the marinade as a sauce.

For a tasty variation, sprinkle toasted sesame seeds on top of the tofu before serving.

Barbequed Tofu

from Nancy Headley
serves 4–6 people

This was the most popular dish at the restaurant that was once operated by the Nyingma community in Boulder, Colorado.

2 lbs	firm tofu

The Marinade:

3 T	peanut butter (or tahini)
⅓ c	vegetable oil
1 T	paprika
¼ t	black pepper
½ t	garlic powder
2 t	salt

Barbeque Sauce:

⅓ c	oil
1	medium onion, chopped
2	cloves garlic, crushed
2½ c	tomato sauce
¼ c	water
½ c	brown sugar
1 T	molasses
½ c	prepared Dijon mustard
1½ t	salt
1 t	allspice
1 t	crushed red pepper (or ¼ t cayenne)
1½ t	dried parsley (or 1 T fresh)
½ c	lemon juice
2 T	soy sauce

Drain the tofu, wrap it in plastic, and freeze until hard—at least overnight. Then defrost it, unwrap it, and squeeze out any water. Cut into chunky strips, roughly ½" x 1" x 2", although the size is not too important.

You can use the time the tofu is defrosting to prepare the barbeque sauce. Sauté the onion and garlic in the oil. Stir in the tomato sauce, water, brown sugar, molasses, mustard, salt, allspice, red pepper, and parsley. Bring to a boil, reduce the heat, and simmer 1 hour. Add the lemon juice and soy sauce, and simmer 10 to 15 minutes more.

Mix the marinade ingredients. Stir the tofu strips in the marinade, and let them marinate for at least an hour. Then lay the tofu strips on an oiled cookie sheet, and bake 25 minutes at 350°. Turn them over, and bake 25 minutes more, until browned.

Pour the barbeque sauce over the tofu strips, and bake another 15 minutes.

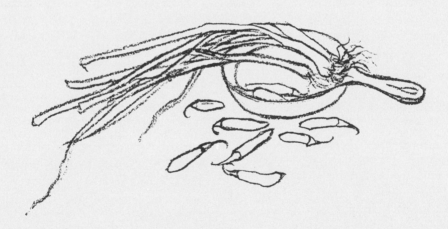

Tofu Fillets

from Zuza
serves 4–6 people

One Nyingma Institute student says these taste like fish. The preparation is easy but takes a little while, due to some waiting time here and there. Plan a lot of extra activity in the kitchen, and return to the tofu every now and then.

2	1 lb packages of tofu
⅓ c	dark sesame oil
¼ c	tamari (soy sauce)
¼ c	rice vinegar
1	red onion, thinly sliced
1 T	ginger
4–5	garlic cloves, pressed

Drain the tofu, and place it on a slanted board so the liquid can drain, preferably near the sink. Cover with another board (I use baking sheets) and weigh it down with a heavy pot to press the tofu. Let stand 30 minutes.

Meanwhile, whisk together the oil, tamari, and rice vinegar. Cut the pressed tofu into slabs, and lay them flat in a shallow glass baking dish. Cover with the marinade. Let stand for another 30 minutes, or refrigerate overnight, turning occasionally.

Heat the griddle or a heavy skillet. Drain the tofu, reserving the marinade. Without adding extra fat, fry the tofu slabs on both sides until crisp and golden brown. Return them to the baking dish. Add the onion, ginger, and garlic to the marinade—then pour it over the tofu, and bake for half an hour in a 350° oven.

Another way to proceed is to add the onion, ginger, and garlic to the marinade just before you pour it over the tofu. In this case, you will need to pay attention while frying so the onion does not burn (ginger and garlic also like to stick); prepared in this way, the fillets don't need to be baked. They can be served immediately, with the reserved marinade spooned over it.

Or you can skip the frying altogether and bake the tofu instead. In this case, let it sit in the *complete* marinade for at least 24 hours, and then bake uncovered at 350° for 45 minutes.

Philippine-Style Black Bean Stew

from Ralph McFall
serves 4–6 people

1½ c	black beans
8 oz	kombu or wakame seaweed
2 T	oil, or more as needed
1	onion
6–8	cloves garlic
1	carrot, sliced
1¼ c	mushrooms, sliced
2 c	chunks of winter squash
½ c	daikon radish, in small chunks
2–3 T	miso
1 t	chili powder
	salt

This is a vegetarian version of a hearty Philippine dish. First wash the beans, sorting them to remove any stones. Cover with water, and soak overnight. The next day, drain them, add 3 cups of fresh water and the seaweed, and cook for 30 minutes. Meanwhile, sauté the vegetables in 2 tablespoons oil, in the order listed. The garlic mellows during the long cooking, so don't be timid about using a lot. When the beans are barely tender, combine them with the vegetables, adding water as needed to keep them from sticking. When the beans taste cooked, but are still firm, add the miso, diluting 2 tablespoons of it in a bit of water. It will keep the beans firm *and* draw a gravy out of them. Simmer the stew 30–40 minutes, adding chili powder and more miso to taste toward the end. If the miso is very mild, add salt to taste. This makes a great dish the next day, too.

Carrot Curry

from Zuza
serves 4–6 people

1	red onion, sliced
2 t	grated fresh ginger root
4 T	butter
2 t	mustard seeds
2 t	turmeric
1 T	whole roasted cumin seeds
1 t	ground cloves
5	cardamom pods
2 lb	carrots, peeled and cut into matchstick strips
3	large potatoes, thinly sliced
1 t	salt
2	bananas, sliced
2 c	orange juice
½ c	currants
	cayenne pepper, to taste
	lemon juice, to taste
1 c	toasted and chopped cashews

Heat the butter in a heavy pot. Fry the mustard seeds, stirring, until they begin to pop. Add onions and ginger; sauté until translucent. Stir in the other spices except salt; stir 2–3 minutes on a low flame. Add carrots, potatoes, and salt. Sauté until vegetables are barely tender, stirring frequently. Add the bananas, juice, and currants. Turn the heat to high, and bring the mixture to a boil; then lower the flame again, and simmer gently until the carrots are tender. Season to taste with cayenne and lemon juice. Sprinkle cashews on top. Serve over Basmati rice, with yogurt on the side.

Mushroom and Chèvre Tart

from Zuza
makes two 9" tarts

The Crust:

1½	*sticks unsalted butter*
2 c	*unbleached flour*
½ c	*whole wheat or graham flour*
½ t	*salt*
	hot water as needed, about ¼ cup

The Filling:

6 T	*butter*
2	*medium yellow onions*
12 oz	*fresh shiitake or other wild mushrooms*
1 lb	*fresh white mushrooms*
1 t	*salt*
1 t	*coarsely ground black pepper*
1 t	*dried thyme, or 1 T fresh*
⅓ c	*fresh dill, finely chopped*
1 pt	*heavy cream*
8	*eggs*
12 oz	*goat cheese, crumbled*
	additional thyme and black pepper, for garnish

To make the crust, use a food processor to cut the cold butter into the flour. When it is the consistency of coarse corn meal, remove it from the processor, add salt and hot water, and quickly mix with your hand until the dough holds together. Let it rest in the refrigerator for 30–60 minutes.

Meanwhile, prepare the filling. Chop the onions coarsely, and sauté until lightly browned, about 12–15 minutes. Slice the wild mushrooms, and add them to the onions. After 5 minutes, add the sliced white mushrooms, salt, and thyme. Sauté uncovered until the mushrooms are tender and almost all the liquid has evaporated. Then add dill, and remove from the heat.

Beat the eggs together with the cream. Add the cheese, mixing it in with a spoon, so that it is still a little lumpy. Add this mixture to the mushrooms. Do not heat any more.

Preheat the oven to 375°. Remove the dough from the fridge, and roll it out or press it into two pie pans. Flute the edges. Bake for 10–12 minutes—do not let the pie shells brown. As soon as they are out of the oven, you can pour the filling in. (If they puff up during baking, pat them down lightly before adding the filling.)

Return the tarts to the oven for 30–40 minutes at 375°. If the filling has not set, but the edges of the crust begin to brown, either cover the edges with foil or turn the oven down to 350° to finish baking. Then sprinkle with thyme and pepper.

Let the tarts rest for a few minutes before cutting. To create a delicious variation, replace the goat cheese with 2 cups of shredded smoked Gouda, and the dill with ⅓ cup fresh Italian parsley, finely chopped.

Banana Curry

from Ruud Lankreijer
serves 2–4 people

2 lb	bananas, preferably green ones
2 T	vegetable oil
1 t	turmeric
½ t	cumin seeds
1 t	salt
⅛ t	cayenne pepper
1 c	yogurt
1 t	curry powder
1 T	lemon juice

Peel the bananas and cut them into 1" slices. Heat the oil in a heavy pot or skillet, add the turmeric and cumin seeds, and fry for 2 to 3 minutes, stirring constantly. Add the bananas, salt, and cayenne, stir (carefully, so the bananas do not disintegrate), and let simmer for 10 minutes on a low flame. Stir once or twice to prevent scorching.

Add the yogurt, curry powder, and lemon juice. Stir once, and simmer for 5–7 more minutes. Be sure not to overcook, or the bananas will fall apart. Taste to correct seasoning.

A Great Way to Use Leftovers

from Frances Strassman
serves 4–6 people

I f you have leftover vegetables—steamed, baked, or even stewed—there is a way to transform them into an appealing quiche-like dish that will taste like a wonderful made-from-scratch entrée even to people who ate those same vegetables the day before.

	leftover veggies
8 or so	*eggs, lightly beaten*
1 t	*salt*
½ t	*coarsely ground black pepper*
	some of your favorite herbs and spices (depending a little on the seasoning, if any, of the leftovers)
1 c	*grated cheddar or Swiss cheese*
	paprika

P reheat oven to 325°. Put the veggies into an oiled baking dish. Combine the eggs and spices. Pour the egg mixture over the vegetables, cover with cheese, and sprinkle paprika on top. Bake uncovered for 30–40 minutes, or until set and golden on top.

Do not be fooled by the simplicity of this preparation. This dish never fails to amaze our guests and residents.

✦ CHAPTER 5 ✦

Grains

Grains are an important part of the vegetarian diet. When we think about wholesome foods, grains easily come to mind. With the obvious exception of white, refined rice and some fast-food parboiled preparations, most grains available in the market have been spared over-refinement, so you can enjoy both their original taste and their nutritional benefits, including high mineral and vitamin content, valuable proteins, and fiber.

Many long-forgotten grains are coming back into vogue with the rising popularity of "health food". In fact, the vegetarian diet is not really a 20th century fad—the enormous consumption of meat is. In previous centuries, traditional staple foods included many non-meat foodstuffs which, combined in certain ways, served as sources of complete protein. Such traditional combinations as corn and milk, rice and beans, and buckwheat and sour milk can still provide us with the essential amino acids we need to produce the same kind of proteins as are found in meat.

Repetitive diets are a common source of poor nutrition. Grains, however, have the potential of adding great variety to our meals. In fact, the possibilities for improvisation are endless. This section offers a few of our favorite grain recipes, along with some basic guidelines for cooking grains.

Cooking Grains

Many people have an aversion to grains, probably from the childhood trauma of being force-fed some overcooked and tasteless gruel. In fact, grains can be delicious even eaten by themselves—when they are properly cooked. Unlike vegetables, grains need just a bit of salt to bring out their flavor. Often that is all they need in order to be deeply satisfying.

Cook grains in a heavy pan with a tight lid. Such a pan is a worthwhile investment for any cook. Its thick bottom will prevent grains from burning. It will also maintain heat better; this is important because part of the cooking process is letting grains rest, covered, with the heat off. And since grains cook in their own steam, a tight fitting lid is essential.

You can cook your grains in two basic ways, by beginning with either cold or boiling water. Some cooks say that the boiling water method results in grains that are moister, while cold water leaves the grains more chewy. This has not been my experience, but perhaps it will be yours. I prefer the hot water method because it is almost foolproof. Another liquid, such as broth or fruit juice, may be used instead of water.

The following is the procedure I use for cooking most grains. (Buckwheat and polenta like to be treated a little differently, as indicated in the recipes in this chapter; for cooking couscous, see page 56.) Put water to boil in a tea kettle. Heat a little oil (one tablespoon or less) in the pot in which you are going to cook the grain. Add the grain and salt (about half a teaspoonful per cup of grain), and sauté over a medium flame for several minutes, stirring frequently (grains burn easily). Add the appropriate amount of boiling water (or whatever liquid you are using), stir once, cover, and turn the flame down to very low. Then leave it alone. *DO NOT EVEN PEEK* before the required cooking time is completed. Never stir grains while they are cooking. When the time is up, lift the pot off the heat *(AGAIN—DON'T PEEK)* and let the grain rest for 5 minutes, covered and unseen. Fluff with a fork before serving.

The "appropriate amount" of water and cooking time vary from grain to grain, and sometimes depend on additional, seemingly mysterious factors. (Perhaps the age of a grain has an effect, or the amount of water it contains when "dry.") The following chart gives approximations, but no guarantees:

Grain (1 c dry)	Water	Time
Brown rice, short	1½ c	50 min
Brown rice, long	1⅓ c	40 min
Basmati	1 c	10–12 min
Barley	2½ c	1 hour
Buckwheat	1½ c	15 min
Polenta	4 c	30 min
Millet	1⅓ c	20 min

Here's a helpful general principle about cooking grains: when you increase the amount of dry grain, the ratio between it and the water changes—that is, the further you venture past one cup of grain, the less water, proportionally, you will need.

Many people have trouble estimating how much grain to prepare. A basic measurement is half a cup of dry grain per person. But don't worry if you make too much: leftover grains have wonderful potential. They can be reheated easily; a small steamer works better than anything—the grains won't scorch, get soggy, or require extra fat. Then salads, pilafs, gratins, and other dishes can benefit from leftover rice, couscous, polenta, and so on. And remember, some of the best breads are made with leftovers.

Polenta Supreme

from Zuza
serves 4–6 people

1½ c	*medium coarse corn meal*
1½ c	*cold water*
4 c	*boiling water*
½ t	*salt*
3 c	*smoked gouda cheese, shredded*
	olive oil

Preheat the oven to 350°. Mix the corn meal with the cold water to make a homogeneous paste. Add boiling water and salt and heat over a medium flame, stirring constantly until it boils. Cover, turn the heat very low, and let simmer for 10 minutes. Then check for doneness. If all the water is absorbed but the grain still tastes raw, add a little more hot water and simmer till cooked.

When the grain is tender and all the water is absorbed, add the cheese. Mix well, and transfer the paste into an oiled shallow baking dish, spreading it evenly. Brush the top with olive oil. Bake for 30 minutes or until golden on top. Remove from the oven, and let stand for 5 minutes. Then cut in triangles, and serve immediately.

For variety, when you add the cheese, mix in chopped fresh cilantro, diced pimiento peppers, diced jalapeño chilies, or whatever else comes to mind that can add color, flavor, or both.

Gourmet Rice

from Frances Strassman
serves 2–4 people

A first-class bowl of rice actually needs no embellishment to be deeply satisfying. When you add a simple salad and a little cheese, a meal cannot get any better. And, if you insist on embellishments, there are many delightful possibilities.

1 c	*long grain brown rice*
½ T	*smoky sesame oil*
1⅓ c	*water*
	small pinch of salt

Stir the rice and oil together until the grains are coated. Sauté quickly over a medium high flame, about 7 minutes. Cool the pan. Then add water, bring to a boil, reduce the heat, cover, and simmer 45 minutes. When you reduce the heat, be sure the rice is simmering or you will need more cooking time.

Here are several suggestions for wonderful variations:

✦ Try adding corn. Boil an ear of corn for 3 minutes, let it cool, and slice off the kernels with a sharp knife. Add the kernels to the rice at the fork-tossing stage, and leave together for 5 minutes in the pan before serving.

✦ Or you could add several of the following: scallion rounds, minced herbs, minced raw red onion, coarse ground black pepper, finely grated orange peel, chopped olives, chopped pimiento, chopped mild cooked chilies, or cooked or raw grated zucchini with a little grated lemon peel. A combination of 4 or 5 of these is nice tossed into the rice, which is then served on a platter and garnished with sliced hard boiled egg.

✦ To 3 cups of hot cooked brown rice, add: 1 cup finely minced Italian parsley, ⅓ cup Braggs Amino Liquid (sounds bad but tastes wonderful), ⅓ cup toasted seeds or nuts, and extra virgin olive oil to taste. Serve the rice on a platter garnished with very ripe chopped tomato.

✦ To 2 cups cooked rice, add: 2 cups milk, 3 whipped eggs, 2 cups New York sharp cheddar (or another cheese of your choice), a pinch of salt, 1 cup chopped scallion, 4 tablespoons chopped fresh basil, 1½ cup chopped nuts and seeds (two or three kinds). Put this mixture in an oiled dish, and bake covered at least ½ hour at 350°, and then bake uncovered for an additional 10 minutes.

Wild Rice with Nuts and Cranberries

from Zuza
serves 6 people

2 t	olive oil
2 c	short grain brown rice
1 c	wild rice
6 c	water
1½ t	salt
1 c	chopped celery
¾ c	dried cranberries, soaked in 1 c orange juice
¾ c	toasted and coarsely chopped hazelnuts
½ t	dried thyme
½ t	dried sage
½ t	coarsely ground black pepper
	more salt, to taste

In a small pot, sauté the brown rice in 2 teaspoons oil. Add 3 cups boiling water with 1 teaspoon salt, stir once, cover, and let simmer for 45 minutes over a very low flame. Remove the rice from the heat, and let it rest for five more minutes. Then check for doneness—it should be soft but still chewy. Fluff it with a fork, and let it stand for a few minutes, uncovered, to release the steam.

In another pot, put the wild rice, ½ teaspoon salt, and 2½ cups cold water. Bring to boiling, cover, and let simmer for 45 minutes. Do not let it overcook; remove it from the heat when the grains are tender but firm, and drain any excess water.

It is good to mix all the ingredients while the rice is still warm. If you use rice boiled in advance, warm it up a little in a steamer or a microwave oven. Toss with all the other ingredients, including the cranberries with the juice. Add salt to taste. Let stand for an hour or so, and serve at room temperature.

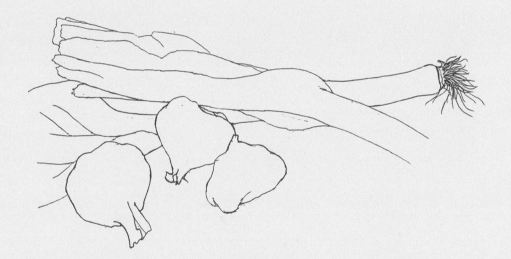

Buckwheat with Dark Mushroom Sauce

from Zuza
serves 4–6 people

If you cannot stand the thought of serving buckwheat groats in your kitchen, try this recipe anyway. This sauce can be also served with pasta; it is excellent in lasagne.

The Sauce:

12	dried mushrooms (shiitake if you can't get porcini)
1 c	Madeira
4 T	butter
1	small yellow onion, finely chopped
4	cloves garlic
1 lb	fresh mushrooms, thinly sliced
1	large red pepper, thinly sliced
4 T	whole wheat flour
½ c	vegetable stock, or more
½ t	salt, or more, to taste
	black pepper, to taste
2 T	soy sauce
1 t	Worcestershire sauce

The Buckwheat:

1 c	toasted buckwheat groats
1	egg, beaten
½ t	salt
1⅓ c	boiling water, or more

H eat ½ cup of the Madeira and pour over the dried mushrooms. Let soak for half an hour.

Melt 2 tablespoons butter in a medium saucepan. Add the onion, and sauté until translucent. Press the garlic, add to the onions, and sauté another minute or so.

Drain the wild mushrooms, reserving the wine. Sliver them, add to the onions, and sauté for 2 minutes. Add the fresh mushrooms, the red pepper, salt, and pepper. Sauté until the mushrooms are tender and most of the liquid is reduced.

In a small skillet, heat the remaining 2 tablespoons of butter with the flour, and cook, stirring, for 2–3 minutes. Then gradually whisk in one half cup of the vegetable stock and the Madeira (include the Madeira in which the mushrooms were soaking, but do it slowly and after you have let it settle, so that any possible sediments are left on the bottom of the bowl). Add soy sauce and Worcestershire. Cook for 10 minutes over medium heat. Add more stock if the sauce is too thick. Correct seasoning, and set aside.

Put the groats in a medium saucepan and add the egg. Stir well to coat all the grains, then add salt and heat slowly. The egg will create a protective shell around each grain, preventing it from falling apart.

When the buckwheat is very hot, add boiling water (be careful—the steam rises quickly and can burn your hand). Stir once, cover, and let simmer, undisturbed, for 15 minutes. Check for doneness—if the grains are still hard and all the water is absorbed, add ¼ cup boiling water. When done, the grains should be tender and should separate easily. (There's nothing worse than overcooked buckwheat. Except for oversalted buckwheat.)

Serve the sauce over the grain, accompanied by a sweet-and-sour salad, such as sauerkraut with carrots and apples.

Bulgur with Nuts and Fruit

from Zuza
serves 4–6 people

Bulgur is parboiled cracked wheat, and it does not need boiling—it will cook when you let it steep in hot liquid. In this recipe, it is cooked first and then baked in the oven with the other ingredients added; the result is a satisfying, lightly sweet side dish. Serve it with baked squash and a green salad.

2 c	bulgur, uncooked
2 ½ c	boiling hot apple juice
1 t	salt
1 t	cinnamon
¼ t	ground cloves
½ t	ground cardamom
2	green tart apples
2	medium-ripe pears
2	stalks celery
½ c	currants, or chopped prunes
⅔ c	toasted and coarsely chopped almonds
2 T	butter
1 c	half-and-half or cream (optional)

In a pot with a tight fitting lid, pour the hot apple juice over the bulgur, add the salt and spices, stir once, and let it steep for 10–15 minutes.

Cut the fruit into ½ cubes, and the celery into smaller ones. Mix these, plus the currants (or prunes) and almonds, into the bulgur when it is done. If the bulgur has absorbed all the liquid and still tastes hard, add a little hot water and let it steep, covered, a few minutes longer before you add the other ingredients.

Place the mixture in an oiled baking dish, dot with butter, and bake at 350° for 45 minutes, or until golden on top. Serve with cream or half-and-half for additional luxury.

Indian Pulao

from Ruud Lankreijer
serves 4–6 people

⅓ c	*oil or butter*
1	*medium onion, finely chopped*
4	*whole cloves*
1 t	*ginger powder*
1 T	*cumin powder*
1 t	*garlic powder*
2 c	*brown rice*
3 c	*boiling water*
1 t	*salt*
1	*2" stick of cinnamon*
	a few shreds of saffron
1 c	*yogurt*

Fry the onion in oil or butter until translucent. Add the cloves, ginger, cumin, and garlic powder along with the dry rice, and sauté 3–5 minutes. Then add water, salt, the cinnamon stick, and saffron. Stir well, turn the heat very low, and let simmer for an hour, tightly covered.

Lift off the heat and let sit 5 minutes, covered. Then fluff with a fork, add the yogurt, and stir. Serve as part of an Indian dinner, or with Lentil Salad and Oriental Carrots.

Millet Cakes with Sun Dried Tomatoes

from Karen Schroeder
serves 4 people

2	cloves garlic, minced
1 T	dried rosemary (or 3 T fresh, minced)
8	sun dried tomatoes
6 T	olive oil
1½ c	vegetable stock
1½ t	salt
⅔ c	millet, raw
2	eggs
6–8 oz	mozzarella, sliced
	pepper, generous grinds to taste

Reconstitute the tomatoes in very warm water to cover, unless they are oil-packed. Drain and chop. In a pot, warm 3 tablespoons oil over low heat, and sauté the garlic for 3 minutes (do not brown). Add the rosemary, and cook 1 minute, stirring. Add the stock and salt, and bring to a boil. Stir in the millet; cover. Cook undisturbed on low heat about 25 minutes, until liquid is absorbed—using a glass pot helps. Then remove from heat, and let stand covered 5 minutes. Uncover and let cool to room temperature.

In a food processor, blend the eggs with *half* the cooked millet until smooth and creamy. Stir the puree into the whole millet, fold in the tomatoes, and add pepper. Form into 8 cakes, about 3" in diameter and ½" thick. In a large frying pan, gently set the cakes in 3 tablespoons very hot oil, lower the heat slightly, and cook, turning once, until crisp and golden brown on both sides (about 10 minutes). Put a slice of cheese on each cake, cover the pan, and remove from heat while cheese melts (about 1 minute).

✦ CHAPTER 6 ✦

Side Dishes, &
Dips & Spreads

Since a vegetarian menu does not really have a main course, then are all of its elements "entrees"? Well, even in such a meal there are additional dishes that fall into the category of "a little something on the side," the topic of this chapter. They tend to be much lighter than an entree, and in most cases quick and easy to prepare. Steamed vegetables, for example, are the simplest. They are always a welcome addition to a meal, providing nutrients, color, and texture, as well as flavor.

Steamed Vegetables

Bring liquid to boil in a pot. Add a steamer and the fresh vegetables, and cover immediately. Prepare the vegetables immediately before steaming to avoid any loss of nutrition. Leave the skins on for the best flavor. Foods can be subtly flavored by adding herbs, onions, and so forth to the cooking liquid. For the maximum flavor, serve immediately after cooking—the peak taste drops off soon. Save the cooking liquids for broth.

Above all, do not overcook. Test for doneness with a toothpick or a thin metal skewer by poking the top of the vegetable or fruit—using a fork instead can cause the juices to run out.

Here are some vegetables (and fruits) to consider steaming:

apples, whole
artichokes
asparagus, whole
string beans, whole
beets, small and whole
broccoli spears
Brussels sprouts, whole
cabbage, quartered
cabbage, small and shredded
carrots, fresh and sliced
cauliflower, quartered
corn on the cob
green pepper, sliced
mushrooms, whole
nectarines, halved
onions, small and whole
peaches, whole
pears, whole
peas
potatoes, small and whole
spinach
tomatoes, small and whole
zucchini, sliced

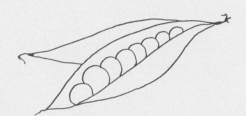

Sauces

....

Steamed vegetables can be served with a variety of sauces and garnishes. The simplest are a little tamari, dried or fresh herbs, or some melted butter mixed with lemon juice. Toasted seeds are great, too—try toasted almonds with a little butter on carrots, walnuts on broccoli, sunflower seeds on Brussels sprouts. Cauliflower and green beans can be served with melted butter and lightly browned bread crumbs. However, use sauces sparingly—when your vegetables are fresh and healthy, their own flavors are entirely satisfying! If you want a sauce recipe, here is an excellent one. Several recipes in this chapter suggest some other ways to prepare vegetables.

Tahini Sauce

from Frances Strassman
serves 4 people

1	*medium white onion, minced*
½ c	*broth*
½ c	*tahini*
2 T	*umeboshi (Japanese plum) paste*
	water

Bring a little water to a boil in a covered sauce pan, add the onion, and cook 4 minutes covered. Spoon the onion into a blender and process for 1 minute. Add the tahini and umeboshi paste, and process 1 minute. Then add the cooking broth slowly and, working with a spatula, process until the sauce reaches the desired consistency. Good on grains and vegetables. If the sauce is too tangy for your taste, reduce the amount of umeboshi paste and increase the tahini.

Side Dishes

Sesame Sweet Potatoes

from Frances Strassman
serves 4 people

3	*large sweet potatoes*
⅓ c	*sesame oil*
⅓ c	*sesame seeds*
	a little salt
	a little oil

Add the sweet potatoes whole and unpeeled to a pan half-full of boiling, salted water. Cook until *just* done, about 15 minutes; when they are done, a metal skewer will slide in without force.

Cool, peel, and cut the potatoes into one inch cubes. At mealtime, sautè the cubes in oil until golden, and add the sesame seeds. (Make extra—these make nice snacks when cold.)

Or cut the potatoes much smaller cubes, cool them, and toss them with salad greens and bits of orange.

New Potatoes

from Frances Strassman
serves 4 people

I s this too simple a recipe? The main secret behind a delightful dish is
not a great number of ingredients or seasonings. It is very fresh, firm
vegetables cooked for the appropriate amount of time. With fresh ingredients and careful cooking, even a simple meal can taste extraordinary.

24	*little new potatoes (with skins)*
¾ c	*milk*
4 T	*butter*
	salt and pepper to taste
	optional: scallions, fresh cilantro, shredded carrots, fresh dill,
	diced pimientos

F or this recipe, scrub the potatoes to remove grit, instead of peeling
them. New potatoes cooked in their jackets for just the right amount of
time have no starchy flavor, and they are a real feast when combined with
just a dab of butter and a grinding of fresh pepper.

Drop the potatoes into boiling water sufficient to cover them. Cook
about 10 minutes, testing for doneness with a toothpick or skewer. Drain
immediately.

With a fork and table knife, lightly chop the potatoes while adding the
milk and butter so both are absorbed and heated. Season with freshly
ground pepper, and add some salt if you wish.

If you would like a fancier dish, add chopped scallion, cilantro, and
shredded carrot after the potatoes are drained, increasing the milk a bit.
This way, the carrots will be both crunchy and hot.

Another serving suggestion: When the potatoes are done, drain them, and leave them whole. Add a handful of chopped fresh dill and 4 tablespoons or so of butter. Salt and pepper to taste. Mild diced pimientos will add an extra touch of color and taste.

Three Things To Do with Squash

Simmered Summer Squash

from Frances Strassman
serves 4 people

3	zucchini squash
3	yellow summer squash
⅓ c	cooking broth
pinch	salt (optional)
1 t	minced parsley

Buy the squash fresh and firm. Slice the yellow squash into ½ inch rounds, and cube the zucchini into ¾ inch cubes. Simmer them together in the broth until just done—about 7 minutes. Drain, and add parsley and perhaps salt. You could serve this dish garnished with a bit of shredded carrot.

Zucchini Sauté

from Frances Strassman
serves 4 people

6–8	small zucchini squash
2 T	your favorite oil

Slice the squash into ¼ inch rounds. Put 1 tablespoon of the oil in a fry pan and heat. Using a medium high flame, add your squash to the hot oil and stir. When all the oil is absorbed and the vegetables begin to stick, add oil as needed, stirring constantly.

The zucchini is most tasty when it has turned a fairly dark brown and you think it is burning. It then has an almost caramel flavor and needs no seasoning or garnish. Very popular!

If you want to gild the lily, add slivered red pepper toward the end of cooking, or toss with pimento. Bits of cooked banana are also excellent. Tossed with shredded sharp Swiss cheese, this zucchini dish is heavenly!

Stuffed Winter Squash

from Frances Strassman
serves 4 people

2	*medium acorn squash*
2	*large Granny Smith apples*
8 T	*tahini*
¼ c	*water*

Scrub rather than peel the squash, since the skin is delicious. Slice the squash in half. Scoop out the seeds.

Core and then cut the apples into halves, top each with 2 tablespoons of tahini, and pack each apple half into the cavity of a squash.

Place the squash in an ungreased baking dish. Pour water in the bottom of the dish, and cover tightly with foil. Bake one hour in an oven preheated to 375°.

Mixed Greens Middle Eastern Style

from Dave Davis
serves 4–6 people

I thought "tasty kale" was an oxymoron until one day Dave served these. Any variety or combination of greens is good in this recipe—collards, kale, beet greens, chard. You can even try including some mustard greens for extra zest.

4	*bunches greens, leaves sorted and washed, stems removed*
2 T	*olive oil*
2 T	*peanut oil*
1	*large onion, chopped medium fine*
8–10	*cloves garlic, minced*
¼ c	*chopped fresh Italian parsley*
¼ c	*chopped fresh cilantro*
2 t	*ground cumin*
2 T	*sweet paprika*
⅛–¼ t	*cayenne (optional)*
1 t	*salt, or to taste*
2 c	*canned tomatoes, chopped, with their juice*

Use a large pot with a tight-fitting lid and a heavy bottom. Coarsely chop the greens. Heat the oil, and sauté the onion and garlic for about 5 minutes, until they are soft. Stir in the herbs and spices, and after a minute or so, add the greens and 1 teaspoon salt. Stir vigorously to mix the greens with the onions and spices. The greens will shrink as they wilt, so you can add them gradually by handfuls if they do not fit into the pot all at once.

Turn the heat to high, and stir in the tomatoes with the juice. Cover and bring to a boil, then reduce the heat to medium. Let simmer, covered, stirring often to prevent sticking. After about 40 minutes, taste for doneness. If the greens are tender, reduce the heat and simmer uncovered, stirring frequently, until they are fairly dry, with only some liquid showing on the bottom of the pot when you stir them aside. Do not leave them unattended until they are finished; they scorch easily, so you need to watch.

Garbanzo Sauté

from Frances Strassman
serves 4 people

2 c	*cooked garbanzo beans, drained dry*
2 T	*your favorite nut oil*
⅓ c	*seeds or chopped nuts*
1 T	*tamari*

Heat half of the oil; then add the beans. Sauté on high heat, stirring constantly, until golden, adding the rest of the oil as needed.

Turn the heat off. Add the seeds or nuts and the tamari. Stir until the beans have cooled and the tamari is absorbed.

Serve with rice pilaf, light salad, and crusty bread—a wonderful light summer meal.

Great as a cold snack, too.

Sweet and Sour Red Cabbage

from Abbe Blum
serves 8–10 people

1	medium red cabbage, shredded
2	green apples (Granny Smith), shredded or finely sliced into small pieces
1–1½ c	chopped prunes
2	medium to large onions, chopped into 1" cubes
¼ c	red wine vinegar
2–3 T	brown sugar, to taste
2 T	oil
1 c	water
1 t	salt

In a heavy saucepan or casserole dish, sauté onions in oil until soft and nearly transparent. Add the apples, and sauté 2 minutes more. If the apples stick, add a little water. Add the cabbage, coat evenly with oil, and sauté for a few more minutes.

Add ½ cup of water, the red wine vinegar, and the brown sugar. Cover and cook, stirring occasionally, for ½ hour. Add the prunes, put a heat deflector under the saucepan, and let the mixture cook down further. Add more water as needed.

The longer it cooks, the softer and more savory the whole dish becomes. Before serving, taste and add more red wine vinegar or brown sugar to taste.

A Gourmet Use of Fruits

from Frances Strassman

Fruits—cooked, raw, or dried—can add surprise to dishes. Have you had green grapes in potato salad? Dried apricot slivers in cole slaw? Pears in spinach salad? Plump baby currants with zucchini? Grated lemon peel with your sautéed platano? What other possibilities come to mind? Be experimental.

Lentil Rolls

from Zuza
serves 4–6 people

1 c	dry lentils
1 c	cottage cheese
1 c	finely chopped red onion
½ c	wheat germ
1 c	soft bread crumbs
½ t	ground cumin
2 t	soy sauce
	chopped almonds, as needed (up to one cup)

Boil the lentils until very tender; drain, and puree when cool enough to handle. Add all the other ingredients *except* the almonds. It is a good idea to refrigerate the mixture for several hours, but this is not essential. Preheat the oven to 375°, and oil a cookie sheet.

Divide the mixture into 10 parts, shape into rolls, and coat each roll evenly with almonds. Place on the baking sheet, and bake 30 minutes, or until golden brown.

Serve warm, and include the leftovers as cold snacks for the next day's lunch.

Homestyle Applesauce

from Frances Strassman
serves 4 people

4	*tart apples*
	water

Chop the apples coarsely, removing the stems and seeds. Place the apple pieces in a very heavy saucepan with a tight-fitting lid. Add water, and bring it to a boil, then reduce the heat to a simmer. Slide a heat deflector under the pot, and cook on *low* heat, stirring occasionally, until the apples are mushy.

If you use fresh fruit of excellent quality, you will not need to add cinnamon or anything else, except perhaps a few grains of salt to bring out the flavors. Try it!

If this seems too radical, put a cinnamon stick in the pot at the beginning, and stir to distribute the flavor.

For an exotic touch, grate a little New York sharp cheddar over the applesauce in its serving bowl.

Dips and Spreads

Hummus

from Zuza
Makes 3½ cups

3 c	garbanzo beans, cooked until very tender
1 c	tahini
3	cloves garlic
	juice of 1-2 lemons
	salt and pepper to taste
pinch	cayenne
⅓ c	cilantro, chopped
1 T	chopped fresh mint leaves

Drain the garbanzos, reserving the liquid. Blend them with all the other ingredients in the food processor, adding the cooking liquid, if needed, to make a thick spread. Leftover hummus can be kept for a few days—and used, for example, as a dip for midnight snacks, with pita bread or crackers.

Guacamole

from Lesley Pulaski
serves 4–6 people

2	*large ripe avocados*
½	*large lemon, juiced*
2–3	*cloves of garlic*
½	*Walla Walla onion (this variety does make a flavorful, crunchy difference)*
dash	*Tabasco sauce*

Mash the avocados with a fork until the mixture is lumpy. Stir in the lemon juice, garlic, onion, and Tabasco.

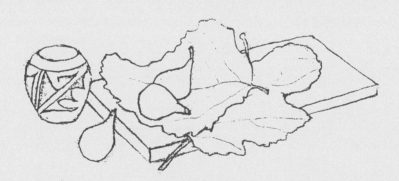

Herbed Cheese Spread or Dip

from Zuza
serves 4–6 people

There is really no recipe for this delicious side dish. The direction it takes depends on which fresh herbs and cheeses you have on hand.

+ *3 cups of any combination of these cheeses: Cream cheese, cottage cheese, ricotta—some goat cheese would make for additional zest*
+ *Up to 1 cup of fresh herbs, finely chopped: dill (definitely!), Italian parsley, oregano, savory, mint*
+ *Fresh lemon juice, salt, and pepper to taste*
+ *Enough yogurt to make the mixture easy to stir and spread, and more if you are making it a dip*
+ *For a crunchy texture and fresh spring taste, add finely chopped scallions (both the white and green parts) and chopped red radishes*
+ *For a hint of Tex-Mex, skip the Italian herbs like savory and oregano, add fresh finely chopped cilantro, and replace lemon juice with fresh lime juice*

Blend together the cheese, lemon or lime juice, salt and pepper, and yogurt; then add the herbs, scallions, and radishes, and mix well.

Tofu Dip

from Zuza
serves 4–6 people

½ c	sunflower seeds
3	cloves garlic
⅛ c	tamari
¼ c	apple cider vinegar
1	block soft tofu
	juice of 2 lemons
	half a bunch fresh dill
4	scallions

In a food processor, process the sunflower seeds and garlic until they become the consistency of coarse meal. Add the other ingredients *except* the scallions, and blend until smooth, scraping the sides of the bowl with a rubber spatula as you go.

Chop the whole scallions, and stir them in by hand—onions tend to become bitter when processed in a machine.

Serve as a dip with raw vegetables and crackers.

✦ CHAPTER 7 ✦

Desserts

The healthiest dessert is a piece of fruit—or better yet, a walk in the woods—but if you want to spoil yourself and your company, choose one of these. When we first started collecting recipes for this book, the ratio of desserts to all other categories was alarming. I was afraid we would end up with a book of 108 gourmet vegetarian desserts. The choice of which ones to include was not easy, but here they are—the best of the best. Some of them are rather rich; reserve those for special occasions. At all cost, avoid serving a heavy dessert with a rich meal. Also, remember while menu-planning that some desserts containing eggs, cheese, and so on are sources of protein and can contribute valuable nutrients to a vegetarian meal.

Polish Poppyseed Cake
(The Lazy Version)

from Zuza
makes two loaves

1 c	black poppyseeds
1 c	milk
2	sticks butter
1½ c	brown sugar
3	eggs
2 c	pastry flour
1 T	baking powder
½ t	salt
¾ c	chopped almonds
¾ c	raisins
1 T	almond extract

In a small saucepan, bring the milk with the poppyseeds to a boil. Take off the burnder, and let cool while you prepare the rest of the ingredients. Preheat the oven to 325°. Butter 2 medium loaf pans, and coat evenly with unseasoned bread crumbs.

In a food processor or a mixer, cream the butter with the sugar. Add the eggs, one at a time. Blend till smooth. In a mixing bowl, sift the flour with the baking powder and salt. Add both the liquid mixtures, alternately, and stir well with a wooden spoon. Do not overmix.

Add the almonds, raisins, and almond extract, and stir briefly. Pour into the prepared pans. Bake 45 minutes, or until golden brown and a knife inserted in the middle comes out clean.

French Pear Pie

from Zuza
serves 4–6 people

The Crust:

1½ c	pastry flour
3 T	sugar
1 t	baking powder
⅛ t	salt
1	stick butter
1	egg
2	egg yolks
½ c	sour cream (or more)

The Custard:

3	ripe pears
2 c	heavy cream
2	egg yolks
2 T	sugar
2 T	brandy (pear brandy, such as Poire Williams, would be ideal)

Sift the flour with the sugar, baking powder and salt. Cut the butter into the flour until it resembles coarse cornmeal. Add the egg and both egg yolks, mix quickly with your fingers, then add ½ cup of sour cream and form the dough into a ball. If it is too dry, add a little more sour cream. Let the dough rest, refrigerated, for at least half an hour. Preheat the oven to 375°.

Roll the dough out to fit into a large pie pan or a 9" x 13" pyrex baking dish. Bake for 10–12 minutes, until pale gold in color.

Meanwhile, prepare the filling. Peel and halve the pears, core them, and sprinkle with lemon juice to keep them from becoming dark. As a decorative touch, use the pointed end of a peeler or grapefruit spoon to carve three evenly-spaced grooves lengthwise along the outside of each pear.

Whisk all the custard ingredients together.

Take the pre-baked crust out of the oven. It will puff up some, but you can tap it back down. Arrange the pears flat side down in a nice pattern, give the custard a last quick stir, and pour it over the pears. Bake at 350° for 30 minutes, or until set and golden on top. Serve either hot or at room temperature.

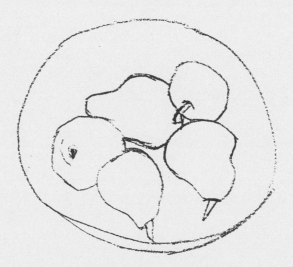

Chocolate Mousse Pie

from Lesley Pulaski
serves 10–12 people

This pie is a special delight. Be warned: it is also elaborate to make and extremely rich. This dessert is best prepared a day in advance.

The Crust:

3 c	chocolate wafer crumbs
½ c	unsalted butter, melted

The Filling:

1 lb	semisweet chocolate
2	eggs
4	egg yolks
2 c	whipping cream
6 T	powdered sugar
4	egg whites, room temperature

The Top:

2 c	whipping cream
	powdered sugar

Chocolate Leaves:

8 oz	semisweet chocolate
1 T	vegetable oil
	waxy, non-toxic plant leaves (e.g., magnolia)

Crust: Combine the chocolate wafer crumbs and the butter. Press onto the bottom and completely up the sides of a 10" springform pan. Chill.

Filling: Soften the chocolate in the top of a double boiler over simmering water. Let cool to lukewarm (95° F). Add the whole eggs, and mix well.

Add the yolks, and mix until thoroughly blended. Whip the cream with the powdered sugar until soft peaks form. Beat the egg whites until stiff, but not dry. Stir a little of the cream and egg whites into the chocolate mixture to lighten. Fold in the remaining cream and egg whites until completely incorporated. Turn this mixture into the crust, and chill at least 6 hours, or overnight.

Top: Whip the cream with sugar to taste, until quite stiff. Loosen the crust on all sides using a sharp knife, and remove the spring form. Spread all but about ½ cup of the cream over the top of the mousse. Pipe the remaining cream into rosettes in the center of the pie. Refrigerate 30 minutes, or chill in a freezer.

Leaves: Melt chocolate and oil in the top of a double boiler. Using a spoon, generously coat the underside of the leaves. Place them on a plate, and chill or freeze until the chocolate is firm. Then separate the chocolate from the leaves, starting at the stem end of the leaves. Arrange the resulting chocolate leaves in an overlapping pattern around the rosettes.

Cut the pie into wedges with a thin, sharp knife.

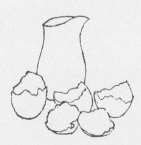

Chocolate Mousse

from Len Hilgerman
serves 6 people

10 oz	dark Belgian chocolate (reserve a little piece for the shavings on top)
4 T	cold water
3 T	sugar
2 t	vanilla
2 T	dark rum
7	large eggs, separated

Luxurious. In the top of a double boiler over hot (not boiling) water, melt the chocolate with the sugar and water. Blend in the vanilla and rum. Allow to cool slightly.

Beat in the egg yolks one at a time, until they are blended. *Then* beat the egg whites until they are stiff, but not dry (to protect them from collapsing, do not beat them until after the yolks are blended). Fold them in carefully.

Pour into soufflé cups. Cover, and chill eight hours, or overnight. Serve topped with a little whipped cream and sprinkled with chocolate shavings.

Plum Pie

from Zuza
serves 4–6 people

The Crust:

3 c	*pastry flour*
5 T	*sugar*
2 t	*baking powder*
¼ t	*salt*
2	*sticks butter*
2	*eggs*
2	*egg yolks*
⅓ c	*sour cream (or more)*

The Filling:

2½ lb	*ripe plums (prunes are also great), halved and pitted*
2 T	*tapioca pearls*
5 T	*brown sugar*
½ t	*ground cloves*

Sift together the flour, sugar, baking powder, and salt. Cut the butter into the flour until the texture of coarse cornmeal. Add the egg and yolks, mix quickly with your fingers, then add ⅓ cup sour cream. Form the dough into a ball. If too dry, add a little more sour cream. Refrigerate for at least 30 minutes. Roll out half, and fit into a 9" x 13" pyrex baking dish. Bake at 375° for 10–12 minutes, until pale golden. Top with the plums, add tapioca, and sprinkle with sugar and cloves. Roll out the rest of the dough for the top crust. Seal the edges of the crust, and prick here and there with a fork. Return it to the oven, baking for another 40 minutes, until golden on top. Let it cool a little. Sprinkle with powdered sugar before serving, or serve with brandied, lightly sweetened whipped cream.

Swiss Lemon Cake

from Ines Hatt
makes one 10" cake

The Cake:
2½   sticks butter
1⅓ c   sugar
5   eggs
        grated rind of 2 lemons
2 c   flour
½ t   baking powder
½ t   baking soda
        pinch of salt
The Glaze:
⅔ c   freshly pressed lemon juice
¾ c   powdered sugar

Be sure not to skip the glaze for this one! The glaze transforms it into a truly *wunderbar* moist cake. To make the glaze, thoroughly mix the ingredients until all the sugar has dissolved.

Preheat the oven to 350°. Butter well a medium loaf pan or a 10" cake form. Cream the sugar with the butter until light and fluffy. Add the eggs and lemon rind. Blend well. Sift the dry ingredients together and fold into the wet mixture. Bake for about an hour.

Let stand in the form for a few minutes to cool, then make deep holes in the cake with a toothpick and pour the glaze over it slowly, so the liquid is absorbed into the cake. Turn the cake out onto a plate, and let it cool completely before serving.

Mocha Cheese Cake

from Fred Lippman
serves 12–16 people

The Crust:

¾ c	graham cracker crumbs
4 t	melted butter
1½T	sugar

The Filling:

1½ lb	cream cheese
1 c	sugar
2	large eggs
8 oz	semi-sweet chocolate, melted in a double boiler
2 T	heavy cream
1 c	sour cream
½ c	pastry flour, sifted
½ c	Kahlua
1 t	vanilla

This is one of my most popular creations. I don't usually like cakes that use alcohol, but the Kahlua really makes this one special.

To make the crust, blend the graham cracker crumbs, butter, and sugar. Press onto the bottom of a springform pan at least 9" in diameter (a little bigger would be better).

To make the filling, beat the cream cheese, sugar, and eggs on low speed. Then increase the speed slowly, and add the chocolate, cream, and sour cream. When smooth, add the flour, and mix thoroughly. Then blend in the Kahlua, and finally the vanilla.

Pour the filling into the crust, and bake at 325° for about 75 minutes, or until settled. Cool and chill before serving.

Sherry Cake

from Abbe Blum
makes 15 to 20 pieces

Although the ingredients are not elegant, the result is a great company cake. I learned the recipe from my high school boyfriend's mother, a remedial reading teacher. I have found that elementary school teachers are often a source of excellent, practical recipes.

⅔ c	*vegetable oil*
⅔ c	*sherry*
4	*eggs*
1	*yellow cake mix (Duncan Hines works well)*
1	*package instant pudding (4 serving size): butterscotch, French vanilla, or vanilla*

Preheat oven to 350°. Grease and flour a bundt cake pan. Using an electric mixer, beat together all the ingredients for 5–8 minutes. Scrape the sides from time to time with a spatula.

Pour the mixture into the bundt cake pan, and bake for approximately 50 minutes, until a toothpick comes out *just* dry. Do not overbake—this cake is better a little moist rather than dry.

Chocolate Port Cake

from Abbe Blum
serves 4–6 people

½ c	port
½ c	butter
3 oz	semisweet chocolate
3	eggs
1 c	sugar
¾ c	flour
⅛ t	salt

Bring the port to a boil. Reduce the heat, and add the butter and chocolate. Melt, blend, and cool slightly. Beat the yolks and sugar, and blend them in.

Let the mixture cool. Then add the flour. In a separate bowl, beat the egg whites and salt until stiff, then fold them in.

Pour into a well-buttered cake form, and bake at 325° for 30 minutes. Let the cake sit until cool. Cut it into wedges or squares, and serve these topped with lightly-sweetened whipped cream and a few strawberries on the side.

Cake Financier

from Ines Hatt
serves 4–6 people

An easy to make coffee cake. As you might guess from the name, this recipe comes from Switzerland.

6	egg whites
1 ⅓ c	sugar
2 oz	blanched almonds, ground
1 t	almond extract
¾ c	all-purpose flour
pinch	salt
1¼	stick butter, melted, at room temperature

Preheat the oven to 350°. Grease a cake pan or a medium loaf pan. Beat the egg whites until very stiff. Add the sugar, and stir briefly. Add all the other ingredients, and mix thoroughly but gently.

Bake for an hour. When Ines served this, she decorated it with little Xeroxed copies of Swiss franc banknotes. You can skip that step.

Mondel Bread

from Evelyn Schieber
serves 4–6 people

2	sticks butter or margarine
3 T	Mazola oil
1 c	sugar, plus 3 tablespoons
3	large eggs (or 4 small)
3 c	flour
2 t	baking powder
¼ t	baking soda
⅛ t	salt
1 t	vanilla extract
1 c	almonds, blanched and slivered
	grated rind of 1 large orange
	grated rind of 2 medium lemons
1 T	lemon juice
2 T	orange juice
1 t	cinnamon

Cream the butter, oil, and 1 cup sugar. Add the eggs whole, one by one, beating after each addition. Sift the dry ingredients together (except cinnamon and extra sugar), and add them, the extracts, and the juices to the first mixture. Refrigerate for 2 hours or more—preferably overnight.

Divide the dough into 6 parts, and form these into rolls 1" thick. Place the rolls on a greased cookie sheet. Mix the cinnamon and extra sugar. Sprinkle half of the mixture onto the rolls. Bake 25 minutes at 350°. Then slice the rolls into 1 inch slices. Place the slices flat on the cookie sheet, and sprinkle the remaining cinnamon-sugar mixture on them. Return them to the oven, toasting them about 10 minutes. Delicious with tea or espresso.

Lemon Cookies

from Zuza
serves 4–6 people

	finely grated rind of 1 lemon
3 T	*lemon juice*
1	*stick butter*
1 c	*sugar*
1	*egg*
2	*egg yolks*
1½ c	*flour*
½ t	*baking powder*
	pinch of salt
½ t	*powdered ginger*

Preheat the oven to 350°. In a small bowl, mix together the lemon rind and the juice, and set aside. In an electric mixer, cream the butter with sugar, add the egg and egg yolks, and beat until light and fluffy.

Sift together the dry ingredients. Add to the mixer, and mix on low speed only until smooth. Add the lemon rind and juice and stir with a spoon.

Line a cookie sheet with foil. Drop the cookies by tablespoonfuls on the sheet, about 2" apart. Place on the middle rack in the oven. Bake for 18–20 minutes, until lightly browned at the edges and firm to a light touch.

Nut & Fruit Drop Cookies

from Evelyn Schieber
makes 108 cookies

½ c	butter, plus some for the baking sheets
1 c	sugar
4	eggs, well beaten
2 t	whiskey or brandy
1 t	cinnamon
½ t	cloves, ground
2 c	flour
1 t	soda in a little hot water
1 lb	English walnuts (2 cups), chopped
¾ lb	pecans (2 cups), chopped
1 c	light raisins
1 c	dark raisins
1 lb	dates, each one cut in 3 pieces

These cookies are rich and satisfying. Cream the butter and sugar. Add the eggs, the whiskey or brandy, the spices, most of the flour, and the soda with water. Then mix together the walnuts, pecans, raisins, and dates, sprinkle them with flour, and add them to the first mixture.

Drop teaspoonfuls of the batter on buttered baking sheets, and bake in a 350° oven for 7 minutes, or until light brown.

Date Balls

from Robin Anderson
makes about 24 balls

½ c	butter
2 c	dates, chopped
2 T	honey
1	egg, beaten
1 t	vanilla extract
2 c	rolled oats (not instant or quick-cooking)
½ c	shredded unsweetened coconut, or as needed

Melt the butter over medium heat. Add the dates, honey, egg, and vanilla. Bring to a boil, and let boil, stirring constantly, for a minute. Pour over the oats while the mixture is still hot, and mix well. Form one-inch balls, and roll them in coconut. Chill and serve.

Low Calorie, Low Fat Dessert Topping

from Abbe Blum
serves 4–6 people

1 c	part skim ricotta cheese
6–7 T	nonfat yogurt
1½ T	honey (or more, to taste)
1½ t	vanilla
¼ t	ginger

Blend all ingredients together in a food processor until very smooth. Use as a topping for fruits such as peaches or strawberries. Also good on cereals.

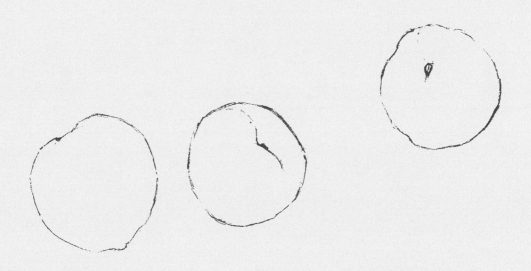

Fruit in Lemon Yogurt

from Zuza
serves 4–6 people

2–3 c	yogurt
	grated peel of 2 lemons
	juice of 1 lemon
1 t	lemon extract
2–3 T	maple syrup
2–3 lbs	red or black grapes

The acidity of the grapes and the yogurt make this dish a wonderful cooler to serve with spicy-hot food. Another acidic fruit, such as strawberries, blueberries, or blackberries, could be used instead of grapes. Or for a dessert, use a sweet fruit, such as bananas or mangos.

It is quick to make. Simply stir the lemon juice, lemon peel, lemon extract, and maple syrup into the yogurt. Then add the fruit.

Strawberries Romanoff

from Mary Webster
serves 4–6 people

½ c	confectioners' sugar
2 pt	strawberries
1 c	whipping cream, whipped
½ t	almond extract
2 T	Cointreau (or orange juice)

Sprinkle the confectioners' sugar over the strawberries. Chill. Then mix with the whipped cream, almond extract, and Cointreau, and serve at once.

Grapefruit Francis

from Mary Webster
serves 4–6 people

1 c	*sugar*
1	*package frozen raspberries, thawed*
8	*grapefruit, sectioned*

Add a scant cup of sugar to the thawed raspberries. Heat, and boil slowly for 10 minutes. Rub through a strainer, and pour over the grapefruit sections.

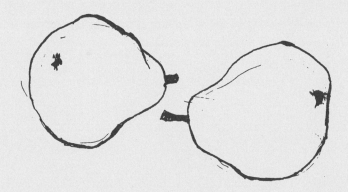

Poached Pears

from Zuza
serves 4–6 people

4	*ripe pears*
1 c	*water*
1 c	*Marsala, port, or sherry*
1	*stick cinnamon*
	a few whole cloves
4 T	*brown sugar*

Peel, quarter, and core the pears. Bring the other ingredients together to a boil, add the pears, and let simmer uncovered for 15 minutes. Let cool slightly or chill before serving. Delicious with lightly sweetened whipped cream.

✦ CHAPTER 8 ✦

Breads &
Breakfasts

This section presents recipes for popular breakfast dishes, especially pancakes, muffins, and breads.

These recipes, as well as a number of recipes from other sections of this book, can be also used when planning a scrumptious brunch menu. Light entrée or side dishes make great additions. Also some desserts, especially fruit desserts, can be adapted to replace the perennial fruit salad, a standard brunch item. Add fresh home made bread, a great treat with any meal.

Here are a few examples of popular brunch menus. In each case, you can expand the menu, adding bread of your choice, and hot and cold beverages. (Have you ever tried Tibetan Tea?)

Grapefruit Francis
Mushroom and Chevre Tart
Fred's Mango Salad

Strawberries Romanoff
Tofu, Mushroom, and Olive Scramble
Potato Pancakes with Blue Cheese

Mango Soup without the Mango
Swedish Pancakes with Brazilian Fried Bananas
Crisp bread with Herbed Cheese Dip

Cream of Asparagus Soup
Wild Rice with Nuts and Cranberries
Salade en Brochettes

Carrot Surprise Soup
French Apple Flan
Banana/Chocolate Chip Muffins

Polish Holiday Vegetable Salad
Tomatoes To Swoon For
Stuffed Baked Pears

Breakfasts

....

Swedish Pancakes

from Marianne Bage
makes 10 to 12 thin pancakes

3	*eggs*
2 c	*milk*
1 c	*flour*
½ t	*salt*
½ t	*sugar*
	butter or margarine for frying

Beat the eggs with ½ c of milk. Mix in the flour, and smooth out all lumps. Add the rest of the milk, plus the salt and sugar, and mix well. Let the batter rest for 10 minutes.

Heat a 9–10 inch frying pan. Put in a small dab of butter or margarine. Let it melt and turn slightly golden, then pour in enough batter to cover ⅔ of the bottom of the pan. Let the batter settle for a moment, then turn the pan so the batter flows out evenly to cover the entire bottom. Turn the pancake when the edges appear light brown and lacy. Let it brown on the other side. Serve hot with your favorite jam.

These pancakes also make a wonderful cake, and give the cook the opportunity to sit down and enjoy a peaceful meal with family and guests. Preheat the oven to 400°. Fry the pancakes as already described. Then stack them on an oven-proof platter, spreading your favorite jam between each layer. Beat together 3 egg whites and ½ cup of sugar until stiff but not dry. Spread this meringue mixture onto the top and sides of the pancake stack. Bake until the meringue turns golden. Serve at once, and enjoy.

Yeasted Pancakes

from Ralph McFall
makes about thirty 3" pancakes

4 c	water
½ t	yeast
1 t	salt
2 c	rolled oats
2 c	whole wheat pastry flour
	butter or margarine for frying

Subtly sweet, moist, and easily digested, these are prepared the night before. Just before bedtime, mix the ingredients in a large bowl. The batter should be a little runny. Cover the bowl, and leave overnight in a place that's not too warm (*i.e.*, not above the stove).

By morning, the yeast will be working well, and will have digested and transformed much of the grain. Add more pastry flour as needed to make a proper consistency—so the cakes hold together, yet aren't too thick.

Heat the butter in a heavy skillet until hot but not brown. Drop the batter onto the skillet by spoonfuls, flattening each to make small pancakes. Fry, turning once, until golden on both sides.

This dish is excellent with the traditional pancake toppings. If you make the pancakes larger, you can use them as wrappers for vegetable fillings. Any extra batter may be refrigerated. In fact, it is often better the following day, though it may need some fresh flour to tone down the sourness.

Mommy's Pancakes

from Elsie McCann
serves 4–6 people

1 c	flour
½ t	salt
1 t	baking powder
	milk
1	egg
2 T	melted butter

Mix together the flour, salt, and baking powder. Add the milk, egg, and melted butter to create a thin paste. The trick is to stir only briefly, even leaving a few lumps. This will make the pancakes very moist and tender. Ladle spoonfuls of the pancake mixture onto a lightly oiled and quite hot griddle. The resulting pancakes should be quite thin; if not, add more milk. Cook just long enough to brown both sides.

Potato Pancakes with Blue Cheese

from Zuza
serves 4–6 people

2 lbs	potatoes, peeled and diced
6 oz	blue cheese, crumbled
½ c	onion, diced
¼ c	fresh parsley, minced
⅛ t	salt
⅛ t	pepper
2 T	olive oil

Boil the potatoes until tender, then mash them. Mix the cheese, onion, parsley, salt, and pepper into the potatoes thoroughly. Shape into 3" pancake patties.

Heat about a teaspoon of oil in a heavy skillet, and cook the patties over medium-low heat until lightly brown, about three minutes per side. Add a little more of the oil as needed. Keep the pancakes in a warm oven until you are ready to serve them.

French Apple Flan

from Len Hilgerman
serves 4–6 people

The Flan:

1¼ lb   crisp eating or cooking apples (peeled, cored, and cut lengthwise in
           ¼" slices, making about 3 c)

3–4 T   butter

¼ c   Calvados (apple brandy), dark rum, or cognac

⅛ t   cinnamon

¼ c   sugar (more if the fruit is tart)

The Batter:

1¼ c   milk and liquid from apples

⅓ c   sugar

3   eggs

1 T   vanilla extract

⅛ t   salt

⅔ c   all-purpose flour, sifted
          powdered sugar as topping

The Flan: Sauté apples in hot butter, browning them lightly. Let them stand in the skillet ½ hour with the brandy, rum, or cognac, cinnamon, and sugar. Substitute this liquid for part of the milk used in the batter.

The Batter: Put all ingredients in a blender in the order in which they are listed, and blend at top speed for 1 minute. Alternate approach: Work the eggs into the flour with a wooden spoon, gradually beat in the liquids and the rest of the ingredients, then strain the batter through a fine sieve.

Pour a ¼" layer of the batter in an 8 cup fireproof baking dish, lightly buttered, or a 1½" deep Pyrex pie plate. Set this over low heat on the stove for a minute or two, until a film of batter has set in the bottom of the dish. Remove from the heat.

Spread the apples over the batter in the dish. Then pour the remaining batter over this. Bake for about an hour at 350°.

The flan is done when it has puffed and browned, and a knife plunged into its center comes out clean. Sprinkle powdered sugar on top just before serving. It need not be served hot, but it is best if still warm. It will sink down slightly as it cools.

This dish can also be made with plums, peaches, nectarines, or a mixture of two. Rhubarb is good, too, but it requires more sugar.

Brazilian Fried Bananas

from Sylvia Lyra
serves 4–6 people

In Brazil, there are many kinds of bananas: silver, gold, earth, water, dwarf, and more. For this popular recipe from southern Brazil, we use *banana da terra*—bananas of earth. These are drier than the bananas found in most American stores. If the bananas you are using are "American," use fewer of them and cut them thicker.

8–12   *very small bananas*
        butter as needed
        white sugar to taste
        cinnamon to taste

Skin the bananas and cut them the long way—in 3 pieces if you are using a dry variety, otherwise in 2 pieces. In a big frying pan over a medium flame, or on a griddle, melt enough butter for frying. Cover the surface with bananas. Add more butter as it is absorbed into the fruit. When the bananas are caramel-brown, turn them over carefully so as not to break them. When they are fried on both sides, they should be browned outside and soft in the middle. Serve them hot, sprinkled with white sugar mixed with a little cinnamon. They are great for breakfast, snacks, or dessert.

In northern Brazil, fried bananas often have slices of a mild cheese melted over them. These can be eaten as they are, or between toast. For dessert, cane sugar is poured over them, which makes them almost too sweet. As a sandwich, these northern fried bananas are called *cartola*, which means an old-style magician's hat. I don't know why they have this name.

Tibetan Tea

from *Odiyan Country Cookbook,* published by Dharma Publishing
serves 2 people

This is a stimulating, warming, and hearty beverage. It is not our usual idea of "tea," nor is it a "soup". Traditionally, Tibetans prepare tea that is fermented and pressed into bricks. It is wonderfully aromatic. Soda is added to this broth to sweeten it, neutralize some of the acid, and provide minerals in the Tibetan diet. A little salt, milk, and fermented yak butter complete this traditional brew. The version that we offer is adapted to appeal to both Tibetan and Western palates, although a salty tea may taste strange to us until we lay aside our preconceptions.

2 c   *water*
1–1½ T *Darjeeling or other black tea*
½ c   *milk, or half and half*
¼ t   *salt*
½   *pinch soda*
1 T   *butter*

Boil the water, and pour it over the black tea. Steep the tea for about 10 minutes. Strain into a blender or small saucepan, and add the other ingredients. Run in the blender for a few seconds, or beat the tea with a wire whisk. Heat in a saucepan until quite hot, but do not let it boil.

Serve immediately—and drink it slowly. Some people enjoy this tea with a little grated nutmeg sprinkled on top. It is delicious any time of day, and especialy good when the weather is chilly.

Breads

....

Wheat Germ Biga Bread

from George Wiegand
makes 2 rounds or 4 baguettes

A*biga* (pronounced bee-gah) is a white, stretchy mass full of bubbles. It waits in your refrigerator, developing subtle flavors, until you add it to your bread dough.

The Biga:

1½ c	*warm water*
2 t	*yeast*
2¼ c	*white bread flour*

The Dough:

7 c	*white bread flour*
1½ c	*wheat germ*
3½ t	*salt*
2½ c	*warm water*
1 T	*yeast*
all the	biga

B*iga:* Whisk the warm water and yeast together, then add flour, and mix with a spoon until uniform. Put into a large container so there will be plenty of room for rising. Keep this in the refrigerator for 2 or 3 days.

Dough: Whisk the flour, wheat germ, and salt together. In another bowl, whisk warm water with yeast. Allow the yeast a few minutes to get moving. Then combine the wet and dry ingredients with the *biga*. Knead until the dough is supple and soft. Add a little water if needed, or more flour if the dough is too sticky.

Allow the dough to rise 2 hours. Push down. Allow to rise 1 hour. Push down, and shape into two rounds, or roll out like sausages into four baguettes. Place on an oiled baking sheet. Allow to rise again until the dough feels relaxed—about 1 hour or less.

Bake at 400°, spritzing with a water sprayer before baking and a couple more times during the first 10 minutes of baking. Baguettes should bake about 25 minutes; rounds, 35–40 minutes.

For a nice variation, substitute polenta for the wheat germ. The bright yellow chunks make a cheerful summer bread.

9-Grain Bread

from George Wiegand
makes two 2-pound loaves

The Sponge:

6 c	*coarse whole wheat flour (winter wheat is best for flavor)*
¼ c	*gluten flour (available in any health food store or section)*
¾ c	*9-grain cereal*
1 c	*water*
1½ T	*yeast*
2 c	*warm water*
1 T	*honey*

The Dough:

2 c	*fine whole wheat flour (spring is best for strength)*
1 T	*salt*
6 T	*oil (safflower, soy, and canola are all good)*
3 T	*honey*
3 T	*malt syrup (corn malt or barley malt)*

This is my favorite of the breads we used to make at the old Nyingma Bakery. It's dense but not dry, and chewy, with a great grain flavor.

Sponge: Whisk the whole wheat flour and gluten flours together. Soak the 9-grain cereal in 1 cup water. Whisk the yeast in 2 cups warm water with the honey. Combine all the remaining sponge ingredients, kneading together into a rough mass. Allow this to rise 2 hours, or overnight, in a cool place.

Dough: Whisk the fine whole wheat flour with the salt. Stir the oil, honey, and malt syrup together, then pour the wet ingredients over the sponge and squish together. Add the flour-salt mixture, and knead the dough until smooth and strong. Add a little water if necessary.

Allow to rise just one hour, shape, and place in two pans. Standard 8 x 4 x 4 bread pans are best. Let rise until just above the top of the pan, then bake at 375° for about 45 minutes, until the loaves are a rich brown on top. When cool, wrap in plastic.

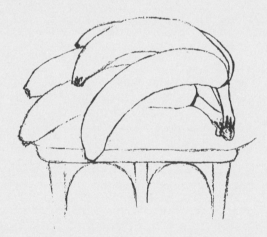

Mashed Potato Bread

from George Wiegand
makes 2 large or 3 small loaves

Using mashed potatoes in bread both uses leftovers and enhances the flavor and texture of the bread. But be sure not to add the potatoes until the dough is already supple, or the result will be a mushy disaster. For dramatic variations, add 2 cups of nuts, cracked wheat, or seeds—*e.g.*, salt and pan-toast chopped walnuts, cool them, and add them to the mashed potatoes.

4 c	*wholewheat flour (or graham flour)*
8 c	*white bread flour*
1½ T	*salt*
3 c	*warm water*
1 T	*honey*
3 T	*yeast*
2 c	*mashed potatoes*

Whisk the flour and salt together in a bowl. In another bowl, whisk the yeast into the warm water and honey. When the yeast begins to foam (after 10 minutes or so), combine the two. Knead into a smooth dough, adding a little water if necessary to make it smooth. Then add the potatoes, and knead until you have a strong but sticky dough. Put this dough in a greased bowl, cover it, and let it stand at room temperature (60°–80°), until the dough has risen and fallen on its own—overnight is usually about right (8 to 12 hours).

Then shape, and bake the dough at 475° for about 25 minutes, first wetting the tops of the loaves with water. Spritz or brush them with water again 5 minutes after baking starts, so the crusts will be brown and crisp. Add a little brown sugar to the water for a multi-colored crust.

Buttermilk Coffee Cake

from Fred Lippman
makes one cake

2½ c	flour
¾ c	sugar
1 c	brown sugar
1 t	nutmeg (optional)
1 t	baking powder
¾ c	oil
1 c	buttermilk
1 t	baking soda
1	egg

Sift together the flour, sugars, nutmeg, and baking powder. Then add the oil. Remove ¾ cup of this crumbly mixture, and set it aside. I like including the nutmeg, but some people prefer the cake without it.

Add the buttermilk, soda, and egg to the remaining mixture, and pour into a pan (about 8" x 10" x 2").

Sprinkle the crumbly mixture over the top and bake at 350° for 45 minutes.

Banana/Chocolate Chip Muffins

from Abbe Blum
makes 10 muffins

½ c	butter
½ c	brown sugar
1 t	baking soda
1 T	hot water
3	bananas, mashed
1	egg
1½ c	all-purpose flour
1 t	nutmeg, ground
¼ t	salt
½ c	chocolate chips

Cream the butter and sugar with an electric mixer. Then dissolve the baking soda in the hot water, and add it, the bananas, and the egg to the butter and sugar, combining them well.

In a separate bowl, mix together the flour, nutmeg, salt, and chocolate chips.

Fold the wet into the dry ingredients, stirring until just mixed. Spoon this mixture into an oiled and floured muffin pan. Bake at 375° for 20 minutes. Remove the muffins from the pan, and let them cool on a rack.

Blueberry Muffins

from Fred Lippman
makes about 1 dozen muffins

3 oz	*melted butter*
1 c	*buttermilk*
1	*egg*
1¾ c	*sugar (vanilla sugar, if possible)*
1 t	*baking powder*
1 t	*baking soda*
½ c	*blueberries*

Begin by melting the butter. Mix in the wet ingredients and sugar, then the dry ones. Spoon the batter into greased muffin tins. Bake at 400° for 25 minutes.

If you think blueberry muffins should have light-colored tops, you might want to put a glaze on them before baking. Either an egg wash (1 egg beaten with 1 tablespoon of cold water) or a dusting of sugar and cinnamon is good.

Index